French Lan  Learning

2 IN 1

French Short Stories for Beginners + French Language for Beginners, Become Fluent in French

By

Language School

French Short Stories for Beginners

Learn French with Short Stories and Phrases in a Fast and Revolutional Way, a Language Learning Book You Will Never Forget

contained within this document, including, but not limited to, —
errors, omissions, or inaccuracies.

Table of Contents

Introduction

Congratulations on downloading *French Short Stories for Beginners: Learn French with Short Stories and Phrases in a Fast and Revolutional Way, a Language Learning Book You Will Never Forget.*

The following chapters will discuss what you should expect from this book, what you can get out of it if used correctly, the best way to use this book to your advantage, and the challenges you might face along with how to approach those issues. The rest of the chapters will revolve around specific settings, allowing you to get a taste of different vocabulary associated with each situation. You will have a mix of dialogue and scenery to familiarize yourself with common words.

The goal of this book is to give you short stories to enjoy and read through, while at the same time having the option to check your own reading against the English translation provided at the end of each chapter. Learning a new language is never easy, but this book can help you continue building up your grammar and vocabulary with fun little stories that incorporate useful every day, words.

There are plenty of books on this subject on the market, thanks again for choosing this one! Every effort was made to ensure it is full of as much useful information as possible; please enjoy!

Chapter 1: What to Expect

In the following chapters, you will find six short stories totaling roughly two-thousand and five hundred words apiece, followed directly by their English translation. These short stories are based around common activities like going grocery shopping, getting your hair done, and taking a trip to the mall. These settings will allow you to learn useful words that you will utilize often in everyday speech.

Chapter Breakdown

Chapter 2 will take you through a trip to the mall between two friends. Common words you will learn from this story include 'shop,' 'price,' 'clothing,' 'cash,' and 'sale.' The dialogue between them will allow you to see how a natural conversation flows between friends, much as you would do when out shopping with your friends. As with all the chapters, there will be a complete English translation to help you along if you get stuck, and to check yourself against.

Chapter 3 will take you on a trip to the grocery store. This story will teach you common words including, but not limited to, 'fruit,' 'meat,' 'canned food,' 'juice,' 'coffee,' and 'vegetables.' This chapter will not only allow you to get a feel for different types of food but also common interactions between the cashier/ store employees and customer, complete with an English translation at the end.

Chapter 4's story shows the common process of getting one's hair done. You will learn common words like 'hair,' 'shampoo,' 'wash,' 'cut,' 'color,' and 'curls.' The interactions between other customers and the customer with her stylist will allow you to see the different ways hair is talked about, and let you relate that for use in your life as you continue your practice. As always, an English translation is at the end for clarification.

Chapter 5's story will take you through a regular morning routine as someone gets ready and heads to work. Dialogue between spouses will enable you to get a feel for the natural flow of conversation while learning common words like 'toothbrush,' 'breakfast,' 'bed,' 'alarm clock,' 'husband,' 'wife,' 'car,' and 'traffic jam.' An English translation can be found at the end to check your work against.

Chapter 6 will take you through a day at the dog park. You will learn common words like 'dog' (male and female), 'grass,' 'fetch,' 'ball,' 'toy,' 'leash,' 'trees,' 'trail' and 'walk.' You will also see common discussions about dogs, a few different breeds, and normal conversation between a couple. An English translation is available at the end for clarification if needed.

Chapter 7 will take you through a dinner party between old friends. You will get to read about the preparation of a meal, a study abroad trip to Australia, and a surprise engagement, along with food dishes and general conversation between multiple people. Common words you will learn in this chapter are 'surprise,' 'study abroad,' 'engaged,' 'streamers,' 'balloons,' 'classes,' 'summer course,' and 'travel.' An English translation is also available at the end if needed.

How to Make the Most of This Book

It is important to keep in mind that everyone learns differently, so the techniques mentioned here may or may not work for you, but they are a good place to start.

It is recommended that you have a piece of paper and a pen or pencil handy, so you can write down any words you are unfamiliar with or phrases you are unsure of. This will make it easier when reading through the English translation so you can quickly find what you were not familiar with instead of having to stop reading, flip to the translation, and then flip back to the French version once you are ready to continue.

While you are reading, do not be afraid to re-read sections that did not make sense. You can even read them out loud to get a feel for the flow a bit easier than just reading in your head. It is recommended that you read through the entire story completely before looking at the translation; this way, you can determine what you actually know without having an idea of the story already in your mind.

Once you have read the story, go through, and read the English translation. While you are doing this, write down the words you did not know, along with any that you may have thought you knew but got wrong. When you have finished reading the English translation, look over your notes for a few minutes, and then re-read the French version again. Keep track of how many of the words you remembered and the ones you are still having trouble with.

Once you have done this, move on to the next chapter and repeat this same process. After you have read the French version a few times, taken note of the words and phrases you were not aware of, have read the English translation and noted the words you were unsure of, and have re-read the French version again, go back to the story you read previously. This can be a useful study tool because once your brain has been thinking about the words of a different story, you will really be able to tell if the words you learned previously are still in your head or if you only remembered them because of how close together you read the English and French versions.

Do not be afraid to make guesses about what you think a word or phrase means. Using context clues, it is possible that even though you do not know a word, you can figure it out by using the words around it. Simply make a note on your sheet of paper about what you think the word/ phrase means, and check it when you get to the English translation at the end. You may surprise yourself! When you do this, you are testing your skills and may even end up giving yourself a confidence boost if your guess was correct.

Learning a new language is never easy, and it does take a lot of practice and dedication on the part of the learner. Time and patience are something you will definitely need in order to master any language, French included, but it is the goal of this book to make your journey a bit smoother.

All of the stories contained within this book are common, everyday events that most people encounter at some point in their life. By using these situations, you will be exposed to words and phrases that are commonplace – and therefore, helpful to you and your studies as they are used frequently.

As with learning anything new, you will hit a few bumps in your studies. These are normal and expected and definitely should not discourage you, though sometimes we know that does happen. If you feel overwhelmed, there is nothing wrong with taking a break and coming back to it later. You can end up stressing yourself out more than necessary if you continue looking at something that does not make sense to you.

With all of this said, hopefully, this book will be able to aid you in expanding and improving your vocabulary and grammar.

Chapter 2: A Trip to the Mall/ Une visite au centre commercial

Claudia et Anna n'étaient pas allées au centre commercial depuis longtemps, mais Anna avait rendez-vous avec Claus, un jeune homme qu'elle avait rencontré au travail, et elle avait désespérément besoin d'une nouvelle robe. Comme les deux femmes étaient les meilleures amies, Claudia est venue avec plaisir.

Les deux se sont rencontrés à l'entrée et se sont serrés dans les bras en se saluant.

"Salut! Comment vas-tu?" demanda Claudia quand les deux femmes entrèrent dans le centre commercial.

"Oh, je vais bien. Je suis juste stressé d'avoir trouvé quelque chose à me mettre." répondit Anna, ses joues un peu rouges. "J'espère qu'on trouvera quelque chose ici."

"Bien sûr ! Nous trouverons certainement une tenue géniale pour votre rendez-vous. Allez, allons voir."

Les deux femmes ont traversé le centre commercial bras dessus bras dessous et sont entrées dans le premier magasin.

Il y avait beaucoup de porte-bagages avec de jolies robes, quelques costumes, des jupes et des chemisiers. Ils ont séparé Claudia à gauche, Anna à droite.

"Si tu trouves quelque chose de bien, prends-le pour moi." dit Anna, une robe déjà sur son bras, "Je les essayerai toutes à la fin."

Claudia hocha la tête et commença à inspecter une étagère. Elle savait qu'Anna voulait quelque chose de spécial parce que c'était son premier rendez-vous avec Claus, et bien sûr, elle voulait faire une bonne première impression.

"Je peux vous aider à trouver quelque chose?" demanda la vendeuse. Elle était petite, blonde et souriante.

Claudia secoua la tête mais indiqua à son amie: "Mais elle pourrait avoir besoin d'aide."

La jeune femme alla voir Anna et lui posa la même question. Anna soupira de soulagement et sourit.

"Oui, s'il vous plaît! Merci infiniment."

"Pas de problème. Je m'appelle Christa. Qu'est-ce que tu cherches?"

Elle soupira de nouveau et regarda à nouveau le support.

"J'ai un rendez-vous..."

Christa sourit en regardant Anna, en toute connaissance de cause : "Avec un homme ?"

Anna hocha la tête, "Notre premier."

"Où vas-tu?"

"Nous allons dîner et assister à un spectacle." J'ai répondu Anna.

"Allez, je sais exactement par où on va commencer." Dit Christa.

Claudia est venue aussi, et les trois dames ont regardé à travers les étagères pour trouver la robe parfaite pour Anna.

"Tiens, essaie ces quatre-là et on verra où on en est." Dit Christa en montrant à Anna les vestiaires.

La première robe était bleu foncé avec des volants et effleurait le sol. Il avait un haut scintillant qui était ajusté et de petits morceaux de paillettes dans la jupe.

"Que pensez-vous de cette robe?" demanda Anna en sortant des vestiaires.
"Oh, c'est une jolie couleur!" s'exclama Claudia.

Christa acquiesça d'un signe de tête: "C'est vraiment bien. Qu'en penses-tu ?"

Anna se regarda dans le miroir, se tournant d'un côté à l'autre. Elle aimait ça, mais elle n'était pas convaincue que c'était *la bonne*.

Claudia l'a senti et a dit:"Essaie les autres, et tu pourras mieux décider."

Anna hocha la tête et entra à nouveau dans le vestiaire.

La deuxième robe était d'un rose pâle, presque corail, et venait juste après ses genoux. Le corsage était lacé dans le dos comme un corset, et la jupe était faite de couches de tulle.

Anna n'a pas aimé celui-ci et a refusé de sortir du vestiaire du tout.

"Ça a l'air ridicule!" se plaignit-elle à travers la porte.

"Oh, allez! Laissez-nous au moins le voir. Tu n'as pas besoin de l'acheter." Dit Claudia, en tapant contre la porte.

"Pas question!" cria Anna en enlevant la robe,"J'essaie la troisième."

"Vous avez aimé le style de celui-là? Peut-être que je peux trouver quelque chose dans une autre couleur." Dit Christa, en venant prendre la robe de l'autre côté de la porte.

"Non, ce n'était pas seulement la couleur. Le style n'était pas pour moi."

Christa est allée remettre la robe rose sur le support pendant que Claudia attendait qu'Anna sorte dans la troisième robe.

"Celui-ci est vraiment joli." Dit Anna, en sortant des vestiaires.

Cette robe était vert émeraude et frôlait le sol comme la première. Cette robe, cependant, avait une sangle et l'autre épaule nue. Il y avait une ceinture de cristal qui s'enroulait juste sous le buste, et la matière était de la soie très douce qui tombait directement de ses hanches.

"Je préfère celui-ci au bleu." dit Claudia, un sourire sur son visage alors qu'elle faisait signe à Anna de faire un tour.

"Tu es magnifique! s'exclama Christa en tapant des mains quand elle revint vers les deux femmes.

Anna hocha la tête: "Je me sens belle dedans."

"Tu veux toujours essayer le dernier?" demanda Christa.

"Oui, dit Anna, mais je pense que c'est la robe."

"Mais ça vaut au moins la peine de l'essayer." Dit Claudia.

Christa a accepté, alors Anna est retournée dans les vestiaires pour l'essayer.

Cette robe était de couleur lavande et plus courte à l'avant qu'à l'arrière. Le devant de la robe était juste en dessous de ses genoux, tandis que le dos touchait presque le sol. Il était fait de satin léger et serré à la taille.

Anna est sortie des vestiaires pour montrer Christa et Claudia.

"C'est joli." dit Anna, en se regardant dans le miroir.

"Mais l'autre est définitivement le gagnant, non?" demanda Claudia.
Elle aimait la robe, mais elle pouvait dire à Anna qu'elle préférait l'autre. A vrai dire, Claudia aussi.

Anna hocha la tête: "Je vais aller avec la robe verte, c'est sûr."

Christa sourit et dit: "Allez-y, changez-vous et rhabillez-vous. je vais prendre une paire de chaussures qui ira très bien avec cette robe."

"Vraiment ? Ce serait génial ! s'exclama Anna en souriant alors qu'elle allait se changer.

Une fois qu'elle était sortie, et que Christa avait remis les deux autres robes sur les étagères, Christa lui a remis une paire de talons étincelants.

"Qu'en penses-tu?"

Anna a regardé Claudia, qui les aimait bien aussi, avant de dire : " Je pense qu'ils sont parfaits. Merci."

Une fois qu'Anna a payé la robe et les chaussures, les deux dames ont quitté le magasin.

"Claus va *mourir* quand il te verra avec ça." Dit Claudia, en joignant les bras d'Anna alors qu'ils se dirigeaient vers l'aire de restauration.

Anna rit en disant: "Je l'espère."

Arrivés à l'aire de restauration, ils ont commandé un hamburger et des frites, choisissant une table près d'une fenêtre pour manger.

"Quel spectacle t'emmène-t-il voir?" demanda Claudia, en prenant un morceau de son hamburger.

"Fantôme de l'Opéra."

"Vraiment? J'ai toujours voulu voir ça! J'aimerais avoir quelqu'un pour m'emmener aux spectacles." Elle a dit en riant.

Anna a levé les yeux et a dit:"Que s'est-il passé avec Michael?"

"Il était ennuyeux."

Pendant un moment, ils se sont tus avant de se mettre à rire tous les deux. Claudia n'a jamais été avec personne pendant très longtemps.

"Tu penses que tout le monde est ennuyeux."

"Je ne veux pas!"

Anna a juste souri en mangeant ses frites, choisissant d'ignorer son amie. Ils savaient tous les deux que c'était vrai, mais Anna savait que Claudia le nierait jusqu'à ce qu'elle soit bleue au visage.

"Dans quel restaurant t'emmène-t-il?" demanda Claudia, changeant ainsi de sujet.

"Je ne sais pas. Il a dit qu'il voulait que ce soit une surprise. Tout ce qu'il me disait, c'était de m'habiller formellement."

"Je croyais que tu détestais les surprises?" demanda Claudia, sourcil levé quand elle prit une autre bouchée de sa nourriture.

"Je le veux." Anna a admis:"Mais il a l'air si excité... je suis prêt à l'accepter."

"Eh bien, je suis sûr que tu passeras un bon moment de toute façon."
Anna acquiesça d'un signe de tête. Elle n'avait pas eu de rendez-vous depuis un moment et elle aimait vraiment bien Noël. Ils parlaient depuis quelques semaines - strictement au travail - quand il lui a finalement demandé un *vrai* rendez-vous.

"Quand est-ce que je pourrai le rencontrer?" demanda Claudia.

"Oh, ne commence pas. Tu parles comme mon père maintenant."

"Hé! Je suis ton meilleur ami. Tu as besoin de mon approbation sur ce type." Elle s'y est opposée.

"Tu sais que je te taquine." Elle gloussa en tapotant la main de Claudia: "Je suis sûre que tu le rencontreras bien assez tôt."

"Oh, allez!" argumenta Claudia,"Je n'ai même pas eu le temps de voir une photo de lui."

Anna soupira mais sortit son téléphone de son sac à main. Après quelques secondes, elle a trouvé une photo qu'elle et Claus avaient prise ensemble pendant leur pause déjeuner.

"Ici, maintenant, tu l'as vu." dit-elle en passant le téléphone à Claudia.

Son amie l'a pris, un sourire sur le visage comme elle a dit, "Il est beau. Vous êtes mignons tous les deux."

Anna a repris son téléphone et l'a jeté dans son sac à main avant de dire: "Je sais. Je le trouve magnifique. Et il a des *muscles* que tu ne croirais pas."

Claudia a ri, finissant ses frites en disant : "*C'est* quelque chose dont je veux une photo."

Les deux femmes ont ri, finissant leurs repas avant de retourner vers l'entrée du centre commercial.
"Aviez-vous besoin de quelque chose pendant que nous sommes ici?" demanda Anna.

Claudia haussa les épaules, "Ai-je besoin de quelque chose? Non. Est-ce que je vais probablement acheter quelque chose? Oui."

Les deux femmes ont ri en entrant dans un magasin de chaussures. Claudia a immédiatement trouvé deux paires de chaussures qu'elle voulait essayer, tandis qu'Anna parcourait simplement les rayons.

Elle n'a jamais été du genre à faire du shopping, à moins que ce ne soit vraiment nécessaire, mais Claudia saisissait toutes les occasions d'acheter quelque chose, surtout des chaussures neuves. Pour cette raison, Anna savait que Claudia achèterait quelque chose. Elle l'a toujours fait.

"Que penses-tu de ça ? demanda Claudia, en s'approchant d'elle avec une paire de baskets roses et dorées.

"As-tu besoin d'une autre paire de baskets?" demanda Anna, essayant de cacher son sourire. "Depuis quand tu fais de l'exercice régulièrement?"

"Non, mais ça ne m'a jamais arrêté avant."

"Je les trouve jolies, mais ne serait-il pas plus logique d'acheter des chaussures de travail? Tu aimes toujours les nouveaux talons."
Claudia acquiesça d'un signe de tête. Elle avait un placard plein de chaussures, et les talons constituaient certainement la majorité d'entre eux.

Claudia est allée essayer l'autre paire de chaussures qu'elle avait remarquée à leur arrivée. Ces chaussures pouvaient certainement être portées au travail; parce qu'elles n'étaient pas aussi hautes ou colorées que les chaussures, elle avait tendance à les porter pendant ses jours de congé.

Celles-ci étaient d'une hauteur modeste en tout noir avec un bracelet à la cheville qui avait un fermoir doré.
"Ça irait bien avec le costume que tu as acheté il y a quelques semaines." Mentionna Anna, regardant Claudia modeler les chaussures pour elle.

Claudia hocha la tête: "Je le pense aussi. Tu crois que je devrais les prendre?"

"Combien coûtent-ils?"

Claudia a levé la boîte pour vérifier l'étiquette avant de dire"50 euros".

"Ce n'est pas mal." Anna dit d'un haussement d'épaules: "Attrape-les. Tu sais que tu vas le faire de toute façon."

Claudia rit, remettant les chaussures dans leur boîte avant de les apporter à la caisse.

"Vous avez certainement raison à ce sujet."

Une fois Claudia payée, les deux femmes ont quitté le magasin et se sont dirigées vers l'entrée.

"Merci d'être venu avec moi aujourd'hui." Dit Anna.

"Tu n'as pas besoin de me remercier. Tu ne t'en serais pas sorti sans moi." Elle plaisantait.

Anna roula des yeux mais rit avec elle.

"Tu as probablement raison." Elle a admis.

Anna n'avait jamais été aussi douée pour choisir des vêtements. Claudia avait toujours été celle qui la dirigeait dans la bonne direction.

"N'oublie pas de m'appeler après le rendez-vous pour me raconter tout ça."

"Tu sais, je le ferai." dit Anna, en faisant un câlin à Claudia avant que les deux chemins se séparent.

English Translation

Claudia and Anna had not been to the mall in a long time, but Anna had a date with Claus, a young man that she met at work, and she desperately needed a new dress. Since the two women were best friends, Claudia gladly came with.

The two met each other at the entrance and hugged in greeting.

"Hey! How are you?" asked Claudia as the two women entered the mall.

"Oh, I am good. I am just stressing over finding something to wear." Answered Anna, her cheeks a bit red. "Hopefully we find something here."

"Of course! We will definitely find an awesome outfit for your date. Come on, let us go look."

The two women walked through the mall arm in arm and went into the first store.

There were lots of racks with pretty dresses, a few suits, skirts, and blouses. They separated Claudia to the left side, Anna to the right.

"If you find something good, grab it for me." Said Anna, a dress already over her arm, "I will try them all on at the end."

Claudia nodded her head and started to inspect a rack. She knew that Anna wanted something special because this was her first date with Claus, and of course, she wanted to make a good first impression.

"Can I help you find something?" asked the saleswoman. She was short with blonde hair and a smiling face.

Claudia shook her head but pointed to her friend, "She might need help, though."

The young lady went over to Anna and asked her the same question. Anna sighed in relief and smiled.

"Yes, please! Thank you so much."

"No problem. My name is Christa. What are you looking for?"

She sighed again and looked at the rack once more.

"I have a date..."

Christa smiled as she looked at Anna, knowingly, "With a man?"

Anna nodded, "Our first."

"Where are you going?"

"We are going to dinner and to a show." Answered Anna.

"Well come on, I know exactly where we will start." Said Christa.

Claudia came over, too, and the three ladies looked through the racks to find the perfect dress for Anna.

"Here, try these four on and then we can see where we are at." Said Christa as she showed Anna the changing room.

The first dress was dark blue with ruffles and grazed the floor. It had a glittery top that was fitted and small pieces of glitter in the skirt.

"What do you guys think of this dress?" asked Anna as she came out of the changing room.
"Oh, that is a pretty color!" exclaimed Claudia.

Christa nodded, "It definitely suits you nicely. What do you think?"

Anna looked at herself in the mirror, turning from side to side. She liked it, but she was not convinced it was *the one*.

Claudia sensed this and said, "Try the other ones, then you can decide better."

Anna nodded and entered the changing room again.

The second dress was a light pink, almost coral shade, and came just past her knees. The bodice laced up in the back like a corset, and the skirt was made of layers of tulle.

Anna did not like this one and refused to come out of the changing room at all.

"It looks ridiculous!" she complained through the door.

"Oh, come on! At least let us see it. You do not have to buy it." Said Claudia, tapping against the door.

"No way!" shouted Anna as she took the dress off, "I am trying the third one."

"Did you like the style of that one? Maybe I can find something in a different color." Said Christa, coming to take the dress from over the door.

"No, it was not just the color. The style was not for me."

Christa went to put the pink dress back on the rack while Claudia waited for Anna to come out in the third dress.

"This one is really pretty." Said Anna, stepping out of the changing room.

This dress was emerald green and grazed the floor like the first one. This dress, though, had one strap and the other shoulder bare. There was a crystal belt that wrapped just beneath the bustline, and the material was very soft silk that fell straight down from her hips.

"I like this one better than the blue one." Said Claudia, a smile on her face as she motioned for Anna to do a spin.

"You look beautiful!" exclaimed Christa, clapping her hands together as she came back over to the two women.

Anna nodded, "I feel beautiful in it."

"Do you still want to try on the last one?" asked Christa.

"Yes," said Anna, "But I do think this is the dress."

"It is worth at least trying it on, though." Said Claudia.

Christa agreed, so Anna went back into the changing room to try it on.

This dress was lavender colored and shorter in the front than the back. The front of the dress came just below her knees, while the back almost touched the floor. It was made of light satin material and cinched at the waist.

Anna came out of the changing room to show Christa and Claudia.

"It is pretty." Said Anna, looking at herself in the mirror.

"But the other one is definitely the winner, right?" asked Claudia. She liked the dress but could tell Anna liked the other one better. To tell the truth, so did Claudia.

Anna nodded, "I am going to go with the green dress for sure."

Christa smiled and said, "Go ahead and change back into your clothes. I am going to grab a pair of shoes that will go great with that dress."

"Really? That would be great!" exclaimed Anna, smiling as she went to get changed.

Once she was out, and Christa had put the other two dresses back on the racks, Christa handed her a pair of sparkling heels.

"What do you think?"

Anna looked at Claudia, who liked them as well, before saying, "I think they are perfect. Thank you."

Once Anna had paid for the dress and the shoes, the two ladies made their way out of the store.

"Claus is going to *die* when he sees you in that." Said Claudia, linking arms with Anna as they headed toward the food court.

Anna laughed as she said, "I hope so."

When they got to the food court, they both ordered a burger and fries, choosing a table near a window to eat.

"What show is he taking you to see?" asked Claudia, taking a bite of her burger.

"Phantom of the Opera."

"Really? I have always wanted to see that! I wish I had a guy to take me out to shows." She said with a chuckle.

Anna rolled her eyes and said, "Whatever happened with Michael?"

"He was annoying."

For a moment, they were quiet before both of them burst into laughter. Claudia was never with anyone for very long.

"You think everyone is annoying."

"I do not!"

Anna just smirked as she ate her fries, choosing to ignore her friend. They both knew that it was true, but Anna was aware that Claudia would deny it until she was blue in the face.

"What restaurant is he taking you to?" asked Claudia, effectively changing the subject.

"I do not know. He said he wanted it to be a surprise. All he would tell me was to dress formally."

"I thought you hated surprises?" asked Claudia, eyebrow raised as she took another bite of her food.

"I do." Admitted Anna, "But he seems so excited...I am willing to go with it."

"Well, I am sure you will have a great time regardless."
Anna nodded in agreement. She had not been on a date in a while and actually really liked Claus. They had been speaking for a few weeks – strictly at work – when he finally asked her on a *real* date.

"When do I get to meet him?" asked Claudia.

"Oh, do not start. You sound like my dad now."

"Hey! I am your best friend. You need my stamp of approval on this guy." She objected.

"You know I am just teasing you." She chuckled, patting Claudia's hand, "I am sure you will meet him soon enough."

"Oh, come on!" argued Claudia, "I have not even gotten to see a picture of him."

Anna sighed but pulled her phone out of her purse. After a few seconds, she found a picture that she and Claus had taken together while on their lunch break.

"Here, now, you have seen him." She said, handing Claudia the phone.

Her friend took it, a smile on her face as she said, "He is handsome. You two look cute together."

Anna took her phone back, tossing it in her purse before saying, "I know. I think he is gorgeous. And he has *muscles* like you would not believe."

Claudia laughed, finishing off her fries as she said, "Now *that is* something I want a picture of."

The two women laughed, finishing their meals before heading back towards the mall's entrance.
"Did you need to get anything while we are here?" asked Anna.

Claudia shrugged, "Do I need anything? No. Am I probably going to buy something? Yes."

The two women laughed as they made their way into a shoe store. Claudia immediately found two pairs of shoes that she wanted to try on, while Anna simply browsed the shelves.

She was never one for shopping trips unless it really needed to happen, but Claudia would take any opportunity to buy something – especially new shoes. For this reason, Anna knew that Claudia would buy something. She always did.

"What do you think of these?" asked Claudia, walking over to her in a pair of pink and gold sneakers.

"Do you even need another pair of sneakers?" asked Anna, trying to hide her smile. "Since when do you work out regularly?"

"No, but that has never stopped me before."

"I think they are pretty, but would not it make more sense to buy work shoes? You always love new heels."
Claudia nodded in agreement. She had a closet full of shoes, and heels definitely made up the majority of them.

Claudia went to try on the other pair of shoes she had noticed when they walked in. These could certainly be worn at work; because they were not nearly as high-heeled or brightly colored as the shoes, she tended to wear on her off days.

These were a modest height in all black with an ankle strap that had a golden clasp.

"Those would look great with the suit you bought a few weeks ago." Mentioned Anna, watching as Claudia modeled the shoes for her.

Claudia nodded, "I think so too. Do you think I should get them?"

"How much are they?"

Claudia lifted the box to check the tag before saying, "50 Euro."

"That is not bad." Said Anna with a shrug, "Get them. You know you are going to anyway."

Claudia laughed, putting the shoes back into their box before taking them up to the register.

"You are certainly right about that."

Once Claudia had paid, the two women left the store and headed toward the entrance.

"Thanks for coming with me today." Said Anna.

"You do not have to thank me. You would not have made it without me." She joked.

Anna rolled her eyes but laughed along with her.

"You are probably right." She admitted.

Anna had never been that great at picking out clothes. Claudia had always been the one to point her in the right direction.

"Make sure you call me after the date and tell me all about it."

"You know, I will." Said Anna, giving Claudia a hug goodbye before the two parted ways.

Chapter 3: To the Grocery Store/ À l'épicerie

Gunter détestait faire les courses. Il y avait toujours trop de monde, et il finissait toujours par partir avec beaucoup plus que ce qu'il avait l'intention d'acheter.

Il supposait que c'était probablement de sa faute s'il n'avait pas fait de liste, mais il ne pouvait pas s'en faire. Il s'est dit qu'il savait assez bien ce qu'il avait à la maison et qu'il réussissait toujours à obtenir ces articles... ainsi qu'une dizaine d'autres dont il *n'avait pas* besoin.

Il a blâmé leur publicité.

Et le fait qu'il ne faisait ses courses que quand il avait faim. Une mauvaise idée? Oui. A-t-il vu cela changer dans un proche avenir? Probablement pas.

Gunter s'est rendu à l'entrée de l'épicerie, prenant un chariot avant d'entrer.

Il s'est immédiatement rendu à l'arrière du magasin, comme il l'a toujours fait, et s'est mis à avancer. Il parcourait généralement toutes les allées pour ne rien rater de ce dont il avait besoin - même si c'est certainement ainsi qu'il a fini avec tant d'articles supplémentaires dans son chariot.

Il n'y avait rien à faire, cependant. Il s'était résigné à partir avec plus qu'il n'était venu pour la seconde où il a décidé qu'il devait aller faire l'épicerie en premier lieu.

Gunter marchait dans l'allée des fruits et légumes, se souvenant vaguement qu'il avait besoin de légumes et de fruits.

Il a choisi quatre pommes, deux pamplemousses, cinq pêches, un sac de raisins et trois bananes, les mettant tous dans son chariot. Il discuta un moment entre mûres et fraises avant de s'installer sur les mûres.

Il s'est ensuite dirigé vers les légumes. Il savait qu'il avait besoin de choux-fleurs, de pommes de terre, d'oignons et de haricots verts, mais il ne pouvait s'empêcher d'ajouter des épinards, de la laitue et des carottes aussi.

Il secoua la tête, n'étant pas impressionné par le fait qu'il ajoutait *déjà des* extras. Cela n'était certainement pas de bon augure pour le reste de ce voyage.

Gunter s'est ensuite dirigé vers les réfrigérateurs. Il avait besoin d'œufs, de beurre, de lait et de fromage à la crème. Après avoir pris ceux-là, il a regardé le yogourt à la fraise et a décidé de l'acheter aussi.

Il cherchait de la saucisse de foie, mais il n'arrivait pas à la trouver. En regardant autour de lui, il a vu une employée remplir les étagères un peu plus loin de lui et a décidé de lui demander.

"Savez-vous où est la saucisse de foie ?"

"Oh, ouais. On vient de le déplacer. C'est juste ici." dit-elle, en montrant du doigt la viande de charcuterie qu'elle stockait.

"Merci." dit-il, l'attrapant et continuant à se frayer un chemin dans le magasin.

Il s'est retrouvé dans l'allée voisine à choisir entre deux sortes de céréales différentes. L'homme à quelques mètres de lui semblait faire la même chose, et au bout d'un moment, ils ont ri tous les deux.

"On pourrait penser que ce ne serait pas si difficile à décider." dit Gunter, en repensant aux options qui s'offraient à lui.

L'homme hocha la tête: "D'habitude, ma copine fait l'épicerie, mais elle n'est pas là pour la semaine."

"Alors, tu es tout seul."

Il rit et accepta, "Exactement. C'est vraiment plus difficile que je ne le pensais."

"Avez-vous essayé celui-ci?" demanda Gunter en montrant une de ses céréales préférées.

L'homme secoua la tête.

"J'essaierais bien." Il m'a encouragé:"C'est une bonne idée."

"Merci," dit-il en prenant une boîte sur l'étagère et en la jetant dans son chariot,"Souhaite-moi bonne chance."

L'homme est sorti de l'allée, laissant Gunter décider de ses propres céréales. Suivant ses propres conseils, il prit les mêmes céréales qu'il venait de recommander et se dirigea vers l'allée suivante.

Il a ramassé des choses au hasard dans les deux allées suivantes - du mélange à gâteau, du chocolat Milka et un paquet de gomme à mâcher.

Dans l'allée suivante, Gunter a ajouté des pâtes et du riz à son chariot, ainsi que quelques boîtes de haricots, du maïs et des haricots verts. Il avait l'intention de faire un ragoût de haricots verts, alors il a aussi pris un pot de cubes de bouillon.

Il a décidé de prendre un paquet de boeuf et s'est assuré d'avoir tout ce qu'il fallait pour son dîner ce soir. Une fois qu'il était sûr, il avait tout ce qu'il voulait dans le magasin.

Il a décidé de se procurer du pain frais et du fromage dans la petite boulangerie de l'épicerie.

Après avoir examiné les options pendant un moment, il avait pris sa décision.

"Je peux avoir quatre petits pains et une demi-livre de brie?"
demanda Gunter au vieil homme derrière le comptoir.

"Bien sûr." dit-il en prenant un sac en papier et en le remplissant
de petits pains avant d'aller chercher le fromage derrière la
vitrine. Une fois qu'il l'avait tranché, emballé et mis dans le sac, il
a tout donné à Gunter.

"Voilà pour toi. Passez une bonne journée."

"Je vous remercie. Toi aussi." Dit Gunter, se dirigeant vers la
section des congélateurs.

Il a pris quelques dîners congelés, des bâtonnets de mozzarella et
de la crème glacée à la vanille avant de finalement se rendre à la
caisse.

La file d'attente était assez longue, mais elle s'est déplacée assez
rapidement, et assez rapidement, il a placé ses articles sur le
comptoir.

"Bonjour! Vous avez tout trouvé? demanda la jeune femme
derrière la caisse enregistreuse au moment où elle commençait à
scanner ses objets.

Il hocha la tête: "Plus que ce dont j'avais besoin, comme d'habitude."

Elle rit, "J'entends cela toute la journée. Tu n'es certainement pas le seul."

"Tu as besoin de sacs?"

Gunter secoua la tête en tirant trois sacs en tissu de son sac à dos: "Non, je les ai."

"Votre total est de 98,45 euros."

Gunter en a sorti une centaine dans les années 20 et les a remises à la caissière.

Une fois qu'elle lui avait rendu sa monnaie, il a poussé son chariot jusqu'au comptoir opposé pour charger ses provisions dans ses sacs. Après quelques minutes, il a tout emballé et a poussé le chariot avec ses trois sacs hors de l'épicerie.

Il a chargé ses sacs sur le panier à l'avant de sa bicyclette et a commencé le retour rapide à la maison.

English Translation

Gunter hated going grocery shopping. There were always too many people, and he always ended up leaving with way more than he had intended to buy.

He supposed that was probably his own fault for not writing a list, but he could not be bothered. He figured he knew well enough what he was out of at home and did always manage to get those items...along with ten or so more that he *did not* need.

He blamed their advertising.

And the fact that he only ever found himself shopping when he was hungry. A bad idea? Yes. Did he see that changing in the near future? Probably not.

Gunter made his way to the grocery store entrance, grabbing a cart before entering.

He immediately made his way to the back of the store, as he always did, and proceeded to work his way forward. He generally walked through all of the aisles so that he would not miss anything he needed – though this was certainly how he ended up with so many extra items in his cart.

It could not be helped, though. He had resigned himself to leaving with more than he came for the second he decided he needed to go grocery shopping in the first place.

Gunter walked through the produce aisle, vaguely remembering that he needed vegetables and fruit.

He picked out four apples, two grapefruits, five peaches, a bag of grapes, and three bananas, putting them all in his cart. He debated between blackberries and strawberries for a moment before settling on the blackberries.

He then made his way toward the vegetables. He knew he needed cauliflower, potatoes, onions, and green beans, but could not stop himself from adding spinach, lettuce, and carrots too.

He shook his head at himself, not impressed that he was *already* adding extras. This certainly did not bode well for the rest of this trip.

Gunter then headed toward the fridges. He needed eggs, butter, milk, and cream cheese. After grabbing those he looked at strawberry yogurt, deciding to get it as well.

He was searching for liverwurst, but could not seem to find it anywhere. Looking around, he spotted an employee filling shelves a bit further away from him and decided to ask her.

"Do you know where the liverwurst is?"

"Oh, yeah. We just moved it. It is right here." She said, pointing next to the deli meat she was stocking.

"Thank you." He said, grabbing it and continuing to make his way through the store.

He found himself in the next aisle deciding between two different kinds of cereal. The man a few feet away from him seemed to be doing the same thing, and after a moment they both laughed.

"You would think it would not be this hard to decide." Said Gunter, looking back at the options in front of him.

The man nodded, "My girlfriend usually does the grocery shopping, but she is out of town for the week."

"So, you are on your own."

He laughed and agreed, "Exactly. It is really ending up being more difficult than I thought."

"Have you tried this one?" asked Gunter, pointing to one of his favorite cereals.

The man shook his head.

"I would give it a try." He encouraged, "It is definitely a good one."

"Thanks," he said, taking a box from the shelf and tossing it into his cart, "Wish me luck."

The man headed out of the aisle, leaving Gunter to decide on his own cereal. Taking his own advice, he took the same cereal he had just recommended and made his way to the next aisle.

He picked up random things from the next two aisles – cake mix, Milka chocolate, and a pack of gum.

In the next aisle, Gunter added pasta and rice to his cart, along with a few cans of beans, corn, and green beans. He was planning to make green bean stew, so he grabbed a jar of bouillon cubes as well.

He decided to grab a package of beef and made sure he had everything for his dinner tonight. Once he was sure, he had everything he continued through the store.

He decided to get some fresh bread and cheese from the little bakery inside the grocery store.

After looking over the options for a moment, he had made up his mind.

"Can I get four rolls and half a pound of brie?" Gunter asked the older man behind the counter.

"Of course." He said, grabbing a paper bag and filling it with the rolls before getting the cheese from behind the glass case. Once he had sliced it, wrapped it, and added it to the bag, he handed everything to Gunter.

"There you go. Have a nice day."

"Thank you. You too." Said Gunter, making his way to the freezer section.

He grabbed a few frozen dinners, mozzarella sticks, and vanilla ice cream before finally making his way to the register.

The line was fairly long but moved pretty quickly, and soon enough he was placing his items onto the counter.

"Hello! Did you find everything okay?" asked the young lady behind the register as she began scanning his items.

He nodded, "More than I needed, as usual."

She laughed, "I hear that all day. You are certainly not the only one."

"Do you need any bags?"

Gunter shook his head, pulling three cloth bags from his backpack, "No, I have got these."

"Your total is 98.45 Euro."

Gunter pulled out a hundred in the twenties and handed them to the cashier.

Once she had given him his change, he pushed his cart over to the opposite counter to load his groceries into his bags. After a few minutes, he had everything packed away and pushed the cart with his three bags back out of the grocery store.

He loaded his bags onto the basket on the front of his bike and began the quick ride home.

Chapter 4: Going to the Hair Salon/ Aller au salon de coiffure

Camilla n'était pas allée au salon de coiffure depuis au moins 5 mois, et elle avait *désespérément* besoin de se faire couper les cheveux et de se faire recolorer. Elle l'avait fait teindre d'un rouge ardent il y a quelques mois, et ne l'avait plus coloré depuis.

Ses racines avaient poussé de quelques centimètres, et la couleur s'était fanée à plus d'orange brûlé. Inutile de dire qu'elle n'était pas la plus grande fan de la couleur ou de l'état de ses cheveux.

Ainsi, elle avait finalement décidé de prendre rendez-vous, s'obligeant à prendre le temps dans son emploi du temps chargé pour se faire plaisir. Tout le monde méritait une journée de détente et de soins, et elle était certainement en retard. Depuis qu'elle avait obtenu sa promotion, elle n'avait pas eu une seconde de libre dans la journée pour *respirer,* encore moins pour prendre quelques heures pour se faire coiffer. Mais peu importe à quel point son travail était exigeant, elle l'aimait.

Elle a enfilé ses bottes, son manteau, son chapeau, son foulard et ses gants avant de sortir de son appartement. C'était un mois de novembre assez froid, et elle était reconnaissante d'avoir décidé de porter des gants lors de sa marche vers le métro parce que même si la marche était courte, le vent était fort.

Camilla descendit les marches du métro, scanna sa carte et se dirigea vers son quai pour prendre le train. Une fois à bord, elle a pris un siège vers l'arrière et a attendu son arrêt.

Le train n'était jamais trop bondé en milieu de semaine, car la plupart des gens étaient déjà au travail, de sorte que le trajet ne semblait pas aussi long que lorsque le wagon était plein.

Bientôt, elle descendit à son arrêt et sortit de la gare. Le vent fort lui a encore frappé les joues alors qu'elle faisait la courte marche jusqu'au salon de Gerhard, à trois pâtés de maisons de là.

Au moment où elle a poussé la porte, son nez était rouge et froid, mais elle était reconnaissante pour la chaleur à l'intérieur.

"Hé, ma belle! Ça fait longtemps que je ne t'ai pas vu." s'exclama Gerhard en la serrant dans ses bras.

Camilla rit et dit: "Je sais. Vous avez certainement du pain sur la planche aujourd'hui parce que mes cheveux sont en désordre! Je n'ai pas été nulle part depuis la dernière fois que tu l'as teint ici *il y a des mois.*"

Gerhard roula les yeux mais prit son manteau, ses gants, son chapeau et son foulard pour la suspendre pendant qu'elle s'asseyait dans son fauteuil.

"Quand je répare ça, tu *n'as pas le* droit de laisser les choses se dégrader à ce point." Il l'a prévenu en regardant ses cheveux.

"Je te le promets." Elle a ri. "J'ai l'impression qu'à chaque fois que je voulais entrer, il se passait quelque chose."

"C'est comme ça que la vie se passe parfois, mais honnêtement, comment as-tu pu laisser les choses aller si mal ?" Il secoua la tête, comme pour se débarrasser de la pensée avant de changer de sujet, "Vouliez-vous refaire du rouge, ou autre chose? demanda Gerhard.

Elle n'était pas tout à fait sûre. Elle discutait de la couleur qu'elle voulait faire ensuite, mais elle n'en était pas vraiment arrivée à une conclusion ferme. Elle s'est dit qu'elle ne pouvait plus attendre.

"Surprends-moi." Elle a dit avec un haussement d'épaules: "Je viens ici depuis des années, tu sais ce que j'aime maintenant."

Le sourire qui a éclaté sur le visage de Gerhard n'avait pas de prix lorsqu'il a applaudi de ses mains dans la joie.

"C'est le rêve de tout styliste!" s'est-il exclamé.

Et c'était vrai, honnêtement. C'était agréable de pouvoir laisser libre cours à sa créativité et de décider, sachant ce qu'elle aimait, quelle couleur et quel style lui conviendrait le mieux.

"Eh bien, je suis contente de faire en sorte que ça arrive pour toi." Elle plaisantait:"Je te fais confiance."

Gerhard hocha la tête, se mit immédiatement au travail, mélangeant ensemble les colorants qu'il voulait utiliser.

Camilla était un peu nerveuse, mais elle pensait ce qu'elle avait dit. Gerhard se coiffait depuis qu'elle est arrivée à Paris il y a 5 ans, et il n'y avait personne en qui elle avait le plus confiance pour ses cheveux. Il faisait un travail incroyable depuis la première fois qu'elle est allée le voir, alors elle n'avait même jamais pensé à chercher ailleurs.

Il était aussi amusant et agréable à côtoyer, alors il a fait en sorte que toute l'expérience se sente moins comme une corvée et plus comme deux amis qui passent du temp's ensemble. Avant qu'elle n'obtienne cette promotion, ils étaient assez proches. Elle était passée plusieurs fois à son appartement pour le dîner, et lui aussi pour prendre un verre ou avant qu'ils ne sortent dîner - elle était loin du chef qu'il était et préférait ne pas avoir à cuisiner en général. C'était plus du genre à manger à emporter.

Quoi qu'il en soit, ils avaient passé beaucoup de temps ensemble, que ce soit chez eux, au restaurant, au cinéma ou dans les parcs, pour se promener avec son chihuahua. Ce n'est que lorsqu'elle a obtenu sa promotion qu'ils n'étaient plus aussi proches. Elle ne l'avait pas vu - dans le salon ou hors du salon - depuis 5 mois, et il lui manquait.

"Comment vas-tu, Gerhard?" demanda Camilla, en s'empêchant de regarder dans les bols qu'il mélangeait. Elle voulait que la couleur soit une surprise, mais elle a dû se forcer à ne pas céder à sa nature curieuse.

"Oh, bien, bien, bien. Le business a été incroyable - mieux que je ne l'aurais jamais imaginé, Cam." Il a jailli, s'arrêtant de son mixage pour lui sourire: " Je ne pourrai jamais assez te remercier d'avoir écrit cet article sur cet endroit. Ça nous a apporté tellement plus de clients."

En toute honnêteté, elle l'avait fait parce qu'elle se sentait coupable d'avoir pratiquement disparu depuis près de six mois. C'était le moins qu'elle puisse faire, d'autant plus que son salon de coiffure *était* vraiment incroyable et qu'elle n'avait jamais vraiment vu quelqu'un en sortir insatisfait de ses cheveux. Si quelque chose n'allait pas bien, Gerhard veillait toujours à ce que ses clients soient pris en charge - qu'il s'agisse de réparer une erreur, de faire le service gratuitement ou de toute autre chose à laquelle il pouvait penser pour faire les choses bien.

"Je suis heureux de l'entendre! Tu mérites vraiment cette reconnaissance. Je n'ai jamais vu quelqu'un partir d'ici malheureux." dit-elle, fière de lui. Il avait démarré son entreprise par lui-même il y a presque 10 ans. Il l'avait littéralement construit à partir de zéro, et maintenant c'était l'un des salons les plus connus de Paris - tout cela grâce à son dur labeur.

Gerhard avait l'air fier quand il s'est retourné pour continuer à mélanger ses colorants ensemble. D'abord, il avait voulu faire la majorité de ses cheveux dans ce même rouge vif, mais il voulait teindre ses pointes d'une belle couleur pourpre. En fin de compte, ce n'est pas ce qu'il a décidé, cependant. Il pensait qu'elle avait eu le rouge depuis assez longtemps et qu'il était temps d'apporter un changement plus radical que les fins violettes.

Pouvoir concrétiser sa vision allait valoir le travail qu'il s'apprêtait à faire. Il savait que cela allait prendre au moins 2 à 3 heures, certainement plus longtemps que ce qu'il avait passé sur ses cheveux quand il les a teints en rouge, mais il avait le sentiment que cela allait finir par avoir l'air incroyable.

"D'accord, es-tu prêt?" demanda-t-il, se déplaçant pour se tenir derrière elle avec son plateau de bols.

Trois bols ont noté Camilla. Trois bols remplis de la nouvelle couleur qui allait être sur sa tête.

"Tu ne deviens pas trop folle, n'est-ce pas?" demanda-t-elle, un peu plus nerveuse maintenant.

"Crois-moi, tu vas l'adorer. Ce ne sera pas plus fou que d'avoir les cheveux roux d'un camion de pompiers."

Elle soupira mais décida de le croire sur parole. Elle lui faisait confiance jusqu'à présent, pourquoi s'arrêter maintenant?

Il a commencé à travailler sur ses cheveux, les deux tombant dans un silence confortable pendant qu'il s'affairait à réparer le désordre sur sa tête.

Après quelques minutes de silence, il a pris la parole.

"Comment va le travail pour toi?"

"Oh, c'est bon. J'ai eu une promotion il y a quelques mois, et ils m'ont tenu occupé."

"Qu'est-ce que tu fais maintenant?" demanda-t-il.

"Je suis le rédacteur en chef maintenant." dit-elle fièrement.
"Pas question! C'est incroyable ", dit-il en la serrant maladroitement dans ses bras autour de la chaise du salon. "Nous devons sortir et fêter ça. Ça fait trop longtemps qu'on n'a pas traîné ensemble."

Camilla a ri et a dit: "J'ai eu cette promotion il y a trois mois, Gerdy. Il semble un peu tard pour célébrer maintenant." Elle a dit, en utilisant son surnom pour la première fois depuis une éternité.

"Ne sois pas ridicule. Il n'est jamais trop tard pour prendre un verre entre amis."

Camilla a roulé des yeux mais a accepté, "Très bien, très bien. Quand êtes-vous libre?"

"Moi? Il semble que je devrais te poser cette question, éditrice occupée. Quand travaille-t-il pour vous? demanda-t-il en souriant.

"Mardi... peut-être vendredi si je peux demander une faveur." dit-elle en pensant à son emploi du temps.

"Vous avez mon numéro. Appelle-moi quand tu veux me voir." dit-il en tapant sur son épaule pour lui faire savoir qu'il avait fini. "Vous resterez assis ici une demi-heure à 45 minutes. Je vais vérifier dans 30 minutes, et on verra où il en est."

Camilla hocha la tête en sortant son téléphone pour vérifier ses courriels pendant qu'elle attendait. Gerhard avait une coupe de cheveux à faire, donc il était avec l'autre cliente pendant qu'elle regardait sur son téléphone. La plupart des courriels provenaient de personnes qui voulaient faire partie du magazine qu'elle a édité, ce qui aurait été bien si l'un d'entre eux avait été vraiment *bon*.

Ils ne l'étaient certainement pas. Il semble que la plupart des soumissions qu'elle a reçues dernièrement étaient inférieures à la moyenne. Elle avait des normes, et elle n'était pas prête à faire des compromis à ce sujet pour faire publier quelque chose. Il y avait beaucoup de gens dans son équipe qui pouvaient écrire de bons articles pour elle, donc ne pas avoir de créateurs en vedette pour la prochaine édition n'allait pas être la fin du monde.

"Quelle belle idée de couleur! s'exclama une fille qui venait d'arriver et qui se faisait aider par une autre styliste.

"Merci, c'était l'idée de Gerhard. Je ne sais même pas à quoi ça ressemble." Elle a admis.

Elle était contente que quelqu'un trouve ça joli. Cela l'a rendue moins nerveuse à savoir si elle allait aimer ça ou non.

"Vraiment? demanda la jeune femme aux grands yeux, je ne sais pas si je pourrais faire ça. Ne pas savoir. Ça a l'air dingue."

Camilla acquiesça d'un signe de tête: " C'est certainement l'une des choses les plus folles que j'ai faites dans ma vie. Ça, c'est sûr."

"Je ne gâcherai pas la surprise, mais crois-moi, ça a l'air *super*."

"Tu crois?" demanda Camilla, résistant à l'envie de trouver un miroir et de voir ce qu'il avait choisi. Elle voulait voir le résultat final pour pouvoir le juger correctement.

La jeune femme hocha la tête et dit: "Certainement. Il te va très bien."

Camilla a utilisé les dix dernières minutes pour lire et relire les courriels qu'elle avait consultés avec peu de chance. Elle était tellement prête à voir à quoi ressemblait cette patience n'était sûrement pas son point fort.

"Très bien, allons vers l'évier." Dit Gerhard, en tapant sur son épaule et en montrant du doigt l'autre côté du salon.
Elle hocha la tête et le suivit, s'asseyant à l'évier et se penchant en arrière pour qu'il puisse se laver les cheveux.

Tandis qu'il lui enlevait la couleur de ses cheveux, elle ne pouvait s'empêcher de se demander à quoi cela allait ressembler. Elle n'avait jamais laissé personne choisir sa couleur de cheveux pour elle, encore moins à son insu.

Néanmoins, elle était excitée de voir ce que Gerhard avait trouvé. Il connaissait son style, et elle avait confiance qu'il avait choisi quelque chose qu'elle aimerait.

Après avoir lavé le shampooing et le revitalisant de ses cheveux, il les a essuyés avec une serviette avant de la conduire à la chaise du salon.

Il l'a empêchée de faire face au miroir et a dit:"La grande révélation va être une surprise."

"Oh, allez, Gerhard. Laisse-moi voir."

"Non." dit-il, en peignant ses cheveux mouillés. Il a pris soin de ne pas laisser des morceaux de cheveux tomber sur son visage.

Il était confiant qu'elle allait aimer ce qu'il avait choisi de faire, mais il voulait qu'elle obtienne le plein effet. Il avait besoin de la sécher et peut-être même de la boucler si elle était assez patiente.

Il ne pariait pas dessus, mais il pouvait espérer. Elle avait toujours détesté se faire coiffer après sa teinture, car elle n'avait pas vraiment envie de quoi que ce soit de fantaisiste. Elle ne s'est jamais vraiment coiffée elle-même, alors elle pensait qu'il était inutile que quelqu'un d'autre le fasse - d'autant plus que cela ne durerait qu'une journée de toute façon, et qu'elle n'était pas prête de le faire elle-même.

"Je vais couper tes culs-de-sac, puis les sécher et les boucler." Dit Gerhard, en sortant ses ciseaux.

"Quoi? Tu vas le faire friser aussi? Je ne veux pas rester ici toute la journée, Gerhard." Elle se plaignait, se tournant pour le regarder.

"Soit tu me laisses la friser, soit tu me laisses t'éclater au Brésil."

"Lequel prend le plus de temps?", lui demanda-t-elle en secouant la tête.

Il souriait:"Choisis ton poison, mon amour."

Elle gémit et s'assit sur la chaise, "Juste la courber."

Il a ri et a commencé à lui couper les culs-de-sac, et à son grand plaisir, il ne lui a fallu que quelques minutes avant qu'elle n'entende le sèche-cheveux s'allumer.

Pendant que la chaleur séchait ses cheveux, elle laissait vagabonder son esprit - encore une fois - sur la couleur ou les *couleurs qu'il* pouvait y avoir dans ses cheveux.

Elle savait qu'il ne serait pas rouge parce qu'elle avait cette couleur depuis un certain temps. Elle était presque certaine que ce ne serait pas non plus une couleur normale. Ni marron, ni blonde, ni noire. Gerhard savait qu'elle était bien trop aventureuse pour ça. Elle espérait que ce n'était pas vert, parce que même si elle était ouverte d'esprit, elle n'était pas sûre d'être *aussi* ouverte d'esprit.

Le sèche-cheveux a été éteint, et Gerhard a commencé à couper ses cheveux pour commencer à les friser.

"Tu sors avec quelqu'un dernièrement ?" demanda Gerhard quelques minutes après avoir commencé les boucles.

Camilla a reniflé et a dit :"Non. Du moins, pas dernièrement."

Il a levé les sourcils:"Ça ressemble à une histoire que je veux entendre."

Elle a roulé des yeux mais a expliqué : " Il y a quelques mois, j'ai commencé à sortir avec ce type - Joseph - et tout était tout à fait normal au début. Il était gentil, il m'apportait des fleurs de temps en temps."

Gerhard hocha la tête pour qu'elle continue à se coiffer.

"Eh bien, tout d'un coup, il commence à devenir *bizarre*. Il a commencé à venir à mon travail avec des fleurs même après que je lui ai dit que ce n'était pas ce que je voulais. Il m'appelait un *million de* fois par jour, et au bout d'un moment, j'ai rompu avec lui."

"Quel sale type." Il a dit:"Il s'est passé quelque chose après que tu aies rompu avec lui?"

Elle haussa les épaules, "Pas vraiment. Il a essayé d'appeler quelques jours après, mais il a abandonné quand il a réalisé que je n'allais pas répondre à ses appels ou le rappeler."

Gerhard a ri et a dit:"Tu sais comment les choisir, Cam."

"Tu n'as aucune idée." dit-elle en riant légèrement avec lui.

Gerhard a fini ses cheveux, ajoutant de la laque comme touche finale, et a ensuite demandé, "Es-tu prêt à voir mon chef-d'œuvre?"

Camilla rit mais hocha la tête, "Certainement."

Il tourna la chaise pours qu'elle soit face au miroir, et son regard de surprise était inestimable.

"Oh, mon Dieu!"

Ses cheveux avaient été teints d'un bleu cobalt profond, les pointes d'un pourpre assez vif. Ce n'était certainement pas un regard qu'elle n'avait jamais eu auparavant.

"J'adore!" s'exclama-t-elle en passant ses mains dans ses cheveux.

Il avait ajouté quelques couches pour encadrer son visage, accentuant ses pommettes, et elle n'arrêtait pas d'y toucher.

Elle ressemblait à une personne totalement différente.

"Tu es un faiseur de miracles, Gerhard." dit-elle, debout sur la chaise pour le serrer dans ses bras.

"Je sais." Il plaisantait:"Je suis content que tu l'aimes."

"Je n'ai jamais douté de toi." dit-elle en riant.

Il a roulé des yeux, "Ouais, c'est pour ça que tu étais si impatient de le voir."

"Tu sais que je ne suis pas une personne patiente." Elle a défendu:"Je savais que ça allait être génial, alors je voulais juste savoir."

Il rit et lui fit un autre câlin avant de lui demander: "Alors, tu aimes vraiment ça? Tu ne dis pas ça pour ne pas me blesser?"

"Je ne le ferais jamais. Tu sais que mon visage me trahit de toute façon. Je suis une terrible menteuse."

"Je suis tout à fait d'accord avec ça." dit-il en souriant.

Il l'a conduite à la caisse pour payer, et avant qu'elle ne parte, il lui a fait la promesse qu'elle n'attendrait pas *des mois* pour le revoir.

"Je te le promets, Gerhard." Elle a dit, en levant les yeux, "Et je t'appellerai plus tard cette semaine pour te parler de cette boisson de fête."

Il lui fit un clin d'œil en lui faisant signe en partant.

English Translation

Camilla had not been to the hair salon in at least 5 months, and she *desperately* needed to have her hair trimmed and re-colored. She had gotten it dyed a fiery red a few months back, and had not gotten it colored again since.

Her roots were grown out a few inches, and the color had faded to more of burnt orange. Needless to say, she was not the biggest fan of the color or the state of her hair.

So, she had finally decided to schedule an appointment, forcing herself to make time in her busy schedule to treat herself. Everyone deserved a day of relaxation and pampering, and she was certainly overdue for one. Since she had gotten her promotion, she had not had a spare second in the day to *breathe,* let alone to take a few hours to get her hair done. But regardless of how demanding her job was, she did enjoy it.

She pulled on her boots, coat, hat, scarf, and gloves before making her way out of her apartment. It was a fairly cold November, and she was grateful for deciding to wear gloves on her walk to the subway because although the walk was short, the wind was brisk.

Camilla walked down the steps into the subway, scanned her card, and headed to her platform to catch the train. Once on board, she grabbed a seat toward the back and waited for her stop.

The train was never too crowded midday during the week, as most people were already at work, so the ride did not seem to take as long as it did when the train car was packed full.

Soon enough, she was getting off at her stop, making her way out of the station. The brisk wind hit her cheeks again as she made the short walk three blocks down to Gerhard's salon.

By the time she pushed open the door, her nose was red and cold, but she was thankful for the heat inside.

"Hey, gorgeous! It has been a long time since I have seen you." Exclaimed Gerhard as he hugged her in greeting.

Camilla laughed and said, "I know. You have certainly got your work cut out for you today because my hair is a mess! I have not been anywhere since the last time you dyed it here *months ago*."

Gerhard rolled his eyes but took her coat, gloves, hat, and scarf to hang up for her as she took a seat in her chair.

"When I fix this, you are *not* allowed to let it get this bad again." He warned as he looked at her hair.

"I promise." She laughed. "It just seems like every time I wanted to come in; something would come up."

"That is how life goes sometimes, but honestly, how did you let it get this bad?" He shook his head, as if to rid himself of the thought before changing the topic, "Did you want to do red again, or something different?" asked Gerhard.

She was not entirely sure. She had been debating about what color she wanted to do next but had not really come to any firm conclusion. Now, she figured she could not put it off any longer.

"Surprise me." She said with a shrug, "I have been coming here for years; you know what I like by now."

The smile that broke out over Gerhard's face was priceless as he clapped his hands together in joy.

"This is every stylist's dream!" he exclaimed.

And it was true, honestly. It was nice to be able to let his creativity out and decide, knowing what she liked, what color and style would suit her best.

"Well, I am glad I am making it happen for you." She joked, "I trust you."

Gerhard nodded, immediately setting to work, mixing together the dyes he wanted to use.

Camilla was a bit nervous, but she meant what she had said. Gerhard had been doing her hair since she moved to Paris 5 years ago, and there was no one she trusted more with her hair. He had been doing an amazing job since the first time she went to him, so she had never even thought about looking elsewhere.

He was also funny and great to be around, so he made the entire experience feel less like a chore and more like two friends spending time together. Before she had gotten this promotion, they had been fairly close. She had been by his apartment for dinner multiple times, and he had been by her apartment as well for drinks or before they went out to dinner – she was nowhere near the chef he was and preferred not to have to cook in general. She was definitely more of a takeout food kind of girl.

Regardless, they had spent a good deal of time together, whether it was at their own homes or out at restaurants, the movie theater, or parks to walk his chihuahua. It was not until she had gotten her promotion that they were no longer as close. She had not seen him – in the salon or out of it – for the last 5 months, and she had missed him.

"How have you been, Gerhard?" asked Camilla, stopping herself from looking into the bowls he was mixing. She wanted the color to be a surprise, but she had to force herself not to give in to her nosey nature.

"Oh, good, good. The business has been amazing – better than I could have ever imagined it, Cam." He gushed, pausing from his mixing to smile up at her, "I will never be able to thank you enough for writing that article about this place. It has brought us so much more clientele."

In all honesty, she had done that because she felt guilty about having practically gone missing for almost half a year. It seemed the least she could do, especially since his salon really *was* amazing, and she had truly never seen anyone leave there unhappy with their hair. If something did not go right, Gerhard always made sure that his customers were taken care of – whether that was him fixing a mistake, doing the service for free, or anything else he could think of to make things right.

"I am glad to hear that! You definitely deserve the recognition. I have never seen anyone leave here unhappy." She said, proud of him. He had started his business by himself almost 10 years ago. He had literally built it from the ground up, and now it was one of the better-known salons in Paris – all because of his hard work.

Gerhard looked proud as he turned back to continue mixing his dyes together. First, he had wanted to do the majority of her hair in that same bright red but wanted to dye her ends a lovely purple color. In the end, that is not what he decided on, though. He figured that she had had the red for long enough, and it was time for a change that was more drastic than just purple ends.

Being able to bring his vision to life was going to be well worth the work he was about to put in. He knew that this was going to take at least 2 to 3 hours, definitely longer than he had spent on her hair when he dyed it red, but he had a feeling this was going to end up looking amazing.

"Okay, are you ready?" he asked, moving to stand behind her with his tray of bowls.

Three bowls noted Camilla. Three bowls that were filled with the new color that was about to be on her head.

"You are not going too crazy, are you?" she asked, a bit more nervous now.

"Trust me; you are going to love it. It will not be any crazier than having a fire engine red hair."

She sighed but decided to take his word for it. She had been trusting him thus far, why stop now?

He began working on her hair, the two falling into a comfortable silence while he busied himself fixing the mess on her head.

After a few minutes of silence, he spoke up.

"How is work going for you?"

"Oh, it is good. I got a promotion a few months ago, and they have been keeping me busy."

"What are you doing now?" he asked.

"I am the lead editor now." She said proudly.
"No way! That is amazing!" he squealed, awkwardly hugging her around the salon chair. "We need to go out and celebrate. It has been too long since we have hung out."

Camilla laughed and said, "I got this promotion like three months ago, Gerdy. It seems a little late for celebrating now." She said, using his nickname for the first time in what felt like forever.

"Do not be ridiculous. It is never too late to have a drink with friends."

Camilla rolled her eyes but agreed, "Fine, fine. When are you free?"

"Me? It seems I should be asking you that question, busy editor lady. When works for you?" he asked with a smile.

"Tuesday...maybe Friday if I can call in a favor." She said as she thought over her schedule in her mind.

"You have my number. Call me when you want to meet." He said, tapping her shoulder to let her know he was done. "You will sit here for about half an hour to 45 minutes. I will check it in 30, and we can see where it is at."

Camilla nodded, taking out her phone to check her emails while she waited. Gerhard had a haircut to do, so he was with the other client while she browsed on her phone. Most of the emails were submissions from people who wanted to be in the magazine she edited, which would have been fine if any of them were actually *good*.

They were certainly not. It seemed that most of the submissions she received lately were below par. She had standards, and she was not willing to compromise on those in order to get something published. There were plenty of people on her staff that could write good articles for her, so not having any featured creators for the next edition was not going to be the end of the world.

"What a cool color idea!" exclaimed a girl who had just walked in and was being helped by another stylist.

"Thanks, it was all Gerhard's idea. I actually do not even know what it looks like." She admitted.

She was pleased that someone thought it looked nice. It made her less nervous about whether she was going to like it or not.

"Really?" asked the young lady, wide-eyed, "I do not know if I could do that. Not knowing. It seems so crazy."

Camilla nodded, "It is definitely one of the crazier things I have done in my life. That is for sure."

"Well I will not spoil the surprise then, but trust me, it looks *great*."

"You think so?" asked Camilla, resisting the urge to find a mirror and see what he had chosen. She wanted to see the finished result so that she could judge it appropriately.

The younger woman nodded and said, "Definitely. It looks great on you."

Camilla used the last ten minutes to read and re-read the emails she had been looking at with little luck. She was just so ready to see what it looked like that patience surely was not her strong suit.

"Alright, let us head over to the sink." Said Gerhard, tapping her shoulder and pointing to the other side of the salon.
She nodded and followed him, sitting down at the sink and leaning back so he could wash her hair.

As he shampooed the color out of her hair, she could not help but wonder what it was going to look like. She had never let anyone pick her hair color for her, let alone without her knowing.

Nonetheless, she was excited to see what Gerhard had come up with. He knew her style, and she trusted that he had chosen something she would love.

After he had washed the shampoo and conditioner out of her hair, he towel dried it before leading her over to the salon chair.

He kept her from facing the mirror and said, "The big reveal is going to be a surprise."

"Oh, come on, Gerhard. Let me see."

"Nope." He said, combing her wet hair. He was careful not to let any pieces of hair fall into her face.

He was confident that she was going to like what he had chosen to do but wanted her to get the full effect. He needed to blow dry it and maybe even curl it if she would be patient enough.

He was not betting on it, but he could hope. She had always hated getting her hair styled after it was dyed, as she had no real desire for anything fancy. She never really styled her own hair, so she thought it was pointless for someone else to do so – especially since it would only last a day anyway, and she was not likely to redo it herself.

"I am going to cut your dead ends and then blow dry and curl it." Said Gerhard, taking his scissors out.

"What? You are going to curl it too? I don't want to be here all day, Gerhard." She complained, turning to look at him.

"You either let me curl it or give you a Brazilian blowout."

"Which one takes longer?" she asked, shaking her head at him.

He smirked, "Pick your poison, love."

She groaned and sat back in the chair, "Just curl it."

He laughed and began cutting her dead ends off, and to her delight, it only took a few minutes before she heard the blow dryer turn on.

As the heat dried her hair, she let her mind wander – yet again – to what color, or *colors* could be in her hair.

She knew it would not be red because she had that color for quite some time. She was fairly certain it was not going to be a normal color either though. Not brown or blonde or black. Gerhard knew she was far too adventurous for those. She hoped it was not green, because though she was openminded, she was not sure she was *that* openminded.

The blow dryer was turned off, and Gerhard began sectioning her hair to begin curling it.

"Have you been dating anyone lately?" Gerhard asked a few minutes after he had started on the curls.

Camilla snorted and said, "No. At least not lately."

At that, he raised an eyebrow, "That sounds like a story I want to hear."

She rolled her eyes but explained nonetheless, "A few months ago I started dating this guy – Joseph – and everything was totally normal at the start. He was sweet, brought me flowers every once in a while."

Gerhard nodded for her to continue as he kept styling her hair.

"Well, all of a sudden, he just starts getting *weird*. He started showing up at my work with flowers even after I told him that was not what I wanted. He called me a *million* times a day, and after a while, I just broke up with him."

"What a creep." He said grimacing, "Did anything happen after you ended things with him?"

She shrugged, "Not really. He tried calling for a few days after that, but he gave up when he realized I was not going to answer his calls or call him back."

Gerhard laughed and said, "You sure do know how to pick them, Cam."

"You have no idea." She said, chuckling lightly with him.

Gerhard finished off her hair, adding some hairspray as the final touch, and then asked, "Are you ready to see my masterpiece?"

Camilla laughed but nodded her head, "Definitely."

He turned the chair so that she was facing the mirror, and her look of surprise was priceless.

"Oh, my goodness!"

Her hair had been dyed a deep cobalt blue, the tips a fairly bright purple. It was certainly not a look she had ever had before.

"I love it!" she exclaimed, running her hands through her hair.

He had added a few layers to frame her face, accentuating her cheekbones, and she could not stop touching it.

She looked like a totally different person.

"You are a miracle worker, Gerhard." She said, standing from the chair to hug him.

"I know." He joked, "I am glad you love it."

"I never doubted you." She said, laughing.

He rolled his eyes, "Yeah, that is why you were so anxious to see it."

"You know I am not a patient person." She defended, "I knew that it was going to be great, so I just wanted to know."

He laughed and gave her another hug before asking, "So you really do love it? You are not just saying that so you do not hurt my feelings?"

"I would never. You know my face gives me away anyway. I am a terrible liar."

"I would definitely have to agree with that." He said with a smile.

He led her over to the register to pay, and before she left, he made her promise that she would not wait *months* to see him again.

"I promise, Gerhard." She said, rolling her eyes, "And I will call you later this week to let you know about that celebratory drink."

He winked, waving at her as she left.

Chapter 5: Getting Ready for Work/ Se préparer pour le travail

Le son strident du réveil de Johannes l'a réveillé, comme tous les matins de la semaine. Il a travaillé comme avocat dans un cabinet d'avocats très prospère, et il y avait été pendant 9 ans. Il avait travaillé d'arrache-pied pour en arriver là où il se trouve maintenant, c'est-à-dire comme associé au sein du cabinet.

Il étouffa un gémissement et se retourna, faisant taire l'alarme avant de se retourner pour embrasser sa femme bonjour. Ce n'est pas parce qu'il aimait son travail qu'il aimait se réveiller à 5 h 30 du matin, 5 jours par semaine.

"Bonjour, Maria."

"Bonjour." Elle marmonnait, essayant de secouer le sommeil de son corps.
Les deux étaient mariés depuis 10 ans et se connaissaient depuis la maternelle. Ils étaient pratiquement inséparables depuis le premier jour de leur rencontre, et cela n'avait pas changé au fil des ans. Ils avaient vraiment épousé leur meilleur ami.

Maria n'avait pas techniquement besoin d'être encore éveillée, mais elle savait que leurs deux enfants se lèveraient probablement d'ici une heure de toute façon.

"Je vais prendre une douche." Dit Johannes, embrassant son front avant qu'il ne disparaisse dans la salle de bain.

Maria a arraché les couvertures de ses jambes, ne prenant pas la peine de faire le lit avant d'aller à la cuisine pour commencer le petit déjeuner.

Leur fille, la plus jeune des deux enfants à l'âge de 4 ans, Britta, traversait actuellement une phase où les seules choses qu'elle voulait manger étaient du yogourt, des nuggets de poulet et des œufs. Cela lui a certainement facilité le petit-déjeuner, bien que Maria ait dû admettre qu'elle craignait un peu que cela ne se poursuive pendant une longue période de temps. Sa fille ne pouvait pas simplement survivre avec des pépites de poulet, des œufs et du yogourt.

Luca, leur fils de 6 ans, par contre, n'avait pratiquement rien qu'il *ne voulait pas* manger. Il semblait être comme Johannes si Maria y avait vraiment pensé. Les deux mangeaient généralement jusqu'à ce qu'ils soient bien remplis. Elle pensait que cela avait beaucoup à voir Luca regarder Johannes manger parce que Maria était certaine qu'il n'avait pas appris cela d'elle.

Elle ne pouvait pas se plaindre, cependant, parce que Luca mangerait plus que volontiers ce que Britta était d'humeur à manger. Néanmoins, elle espérait que sa fille se remettrait bientôt à étendre son régime alimentaire. Il n'y avait que si longtemps qu'elle pouvait justifier de lui donner trois aliments ou de discuter avec elle au sujet de la consommation de ses légumes.

Alors que Maria commençait à préparer le petit déjeuner pour le reste de la famille, Johannes se préparait pour le travail.

Il avait fini de se doucher, de se laver et de revitaliser les cheveux, et il portait maintenant son pantalon de travail et une chemise bleue boutonnée, sa cravate grise lâche autour du cou pendant qu'il pressait du dentifrice sur sa brosse à dents et se brossait les dents.

Il s'est rapidement brossé les cheveux et a enfilé ses chaussures, ses chaussettes et sa cravate alors qu'il sortait de leur chambre et descendait le couloir dans la chambre de leurs enfants pour les réveiller.

À sa grande surprise, cependant, ni l'un ni l'autre n'étaient encore dans leur lit, mais ils n'étaient toujours pas faits. Quand il est entré dans la cuisine, il a vu pourquoi.

Britta et Luca étaient assises dans les hauts tabourets qui bordaient l'îlot de la cuisine et regardaient Maria finir son petit déjeuner. Luca et Britta se parlaient tranquillement. On aurait dit que Luca racontait à sa petite sœur ce qu'était l'école. Il allait commencer le CE1 en août, et il semblait que Britta avait beaucoup de questions à ce sujet.

"Tu vas encore voir tes amis ?" demanda Britta, les yeux grand ouverts en regardant son frère.

"Bien sûr." Il répondit facilement : "Nous sommes dans la même classe."

"Et ils le seront pendant quelques années." Maria a ajouté : "Ce n'est qu'au collège que tu pourrais avoir quelques classes sans certaines d'entre elles."

Les yeux de Britta s'élargirent quand elle regarda entre son frère aîné et sa mère en lui demandant : "Que veux-tu dire ? Ils vont te manquer ?"

Luca rit et dit : "Ce n'est pas comme si je ne les reverrais plus. On a plus d'enseignants qu'un seul quand on va à la grande école."

Maria acquiesça d'un signe de tête et Britta sembla réfléchir attentivement à leurs paroles avant de répondre.

"Alors, qu'est-ce que tu apprends à l'école, Luca ?" demanda-t-elle.

"Beaucoup de choses différentes. On apprend l'orthographe, l'écriture et les maths, comme l'addition et la soustraction, et la science aussi." Il m'a expliqué avec un sourire. Il était manifestement fier de ce qu'il avait appris.

"Je veux apprendre à épeler aussi, maman." dit-elle, regardant Maria avec impatience.

Maria gloussa et dit : "Tu sais déjà épeler ton nom, Britta. Tu apprends à épeler."

Cette réponse semblait apaiser Britta, alors elle et Luca se tournèrent vers leur mère.

Maria avait fait des œufs, du bacon et des petits pains beurrés ; tout cela sentait bon. Johannes jeta un coup d'œil à l'horloge de la cuisine et se rendit compte qu'il n'avait que 15 minutes pour manger avant de devoir partir. C'était une garantie qu'il serait coincé dans la circulation aux heures de pointe à 7 heures du matin - ce qu'il détestait. Ils vivaient à environ une heure du cabinet d'avocats, mais avec le trafic, cela prenait parfois plus d'une heure et demie.

Maria et lui avaient parlé de se rapprocher de la ville, et il espérait qu'ils le feraient. Ce n'était pas seulement qu'il serait plus proche de son travail, mais les écoles de la ville étaient meilleures que la campagne où ils vivent maintenant. Ce n'était pas nécessairement que les écoles où ils vivaient étaient *mauvaises* ; elles n'étaient simplement pas aussi bonnes que celles qui étaient plus proches de la ville.

Luca commençait l'école primaire en août, et Britta allait commencer la maternelle dans quelques années, alors Johannes et Maria voulaient tous les deux qu'ils soient dans les meilleures écoles possibles. Ils croyaient fermement en l'éducation - ils avaient tous deux grandi dans de grandes écoles - alors ils voulaient donner la même chance à leurs enfants.

Se rapprocher de la ville permettrait aussi à Johannes de passer plus de temps avec la famille en ne devant pas partir si tôt et rentrer à la maison si tard. C'était typique qu'à son retour à la maison vers 20 h, Britta et Luca étaient tous les deux endormis dans leur lit. Le seul jour où Maria leur a permis d'*essayer de* rester éveillés était le vendredi, mais même à ce moment-là, il était peu probable que l'un ou l'autre des enfants puisse rester éveillé assez longtemps pour le voir. Luca l'avait fait deux ou trois fois, tandis que Britta n'avait jamais réussi à garder les yeux ouverts après 19:00.

Et bien sûr, après une journée entière à s'occuper de Luca et Britta, Maria était épuisée. Comme c'était les vacances d'été, les deux enfants étaient à la maison, pas seulement Britta, alors Maria passait ses journées à faire la lessive, à leur apprendre des choses simples et à jouer avec eux tout au long de la journée. Elle aimait pouvoir s'occuper de ses enfants, de sorte qu'ils n'avaient pas besoin d'aller à la garderie, mais elle ne pouvait nier le fait que c'était beaucoup de travail.

Elle dînait toujours prête et l'attendait au micro-ondes, mais il la trouvait souvent endormie, soit sur le canapé si elle avait l'intention de l'attendre, soit au lit, si elle savait déjà combien elle était fatiguée. Il ne lui en voulait pas du tout. En fait, il savait qu'il était incroyablement chanceux d'avoir une femme comme elle qui était prête à faire tant pour la famille. Il n'aurait jamais pensé pouvoir trouver une femme comme elle, mais il l'avait fait. Il lui serait reconnaissant pour toujours. Non seulement elle lui a donné deux beaux enfants, mais elle a travaillé aussi dur que lui, sinon *plus*. Il savait que Britta et Luca étaient une poignée de personnes et qu'elle devait s'en occuper 5 jours par semaine, toute la journée, mais elle ne s'en est jamais plainte.

"Eh bien, bonjour." Il dit, froissant les cheveux de chacun de ses enfants : "Comment vont mes petits oiseaux ?"

"Ils lui ont dit à l'unisson, lui souriant avant de suivre les instructions de leur mère d'aller s'asseoir à table.

Luca a aidé Britta à s'asseoir sur sa chaise - toujours le grand frère protecteur et serviable - avant de s'asseoir.

Johannes a aidé sa femme à porter la nourriture sur la table, la répartissant entre les quatre avant que les deux parents ne se joignent à la table pour manger aussi.

"Qu'est-ce qu'on dit à maman ?" demanda Johannes à ses deux enfants.

"Merci, maman !" ils se sont fait l'écho l'un de l'autre en souriant.

Maria sourit et mit un peu de tout sur les assiettes de Luca et Britta, coupant leurs petits pains en deux et les beurrant pour eux, avant de les déposer à nouveau devant chaque enfant.

"Laisse-moi réparer ton assiette." dit Johannes, lui remettant déjà une assiette remplie avec le sourire.

Elle n'a pas pu s'empêcher de sourire et a pris la nourriture avec un merci.

"Y a-t-il quelque chose d'intéressant au travail aujourd'hui ? demanda Maria, en prenant une gorgée de son café.

Johannes haussa les épaules, "Nulle part aussi intéressant que je suis sûr que ce sera ici."

Britta frappa des mains en souriant, mais c'est Luca qui parla plus fort.

"Non ! Le travail est ennuyeux, papa."

Johannes gloussa, froissant de nouveau les cheveux de son fils avant de dire : "En fait, je suis d'accord avec vous."

"Est-ce que Fredrich a fini par avoir cette affaire très médiatisée que vous cherchiez ?" demanda Maria, en prenant une bouchée de ses oeufs.

Johannes hocha la tête, et après avoir pris une gorgée de son café, il dit : "Oui, j'ai été assez surpris. L'autre cabinet d'avocats qui voulait cette affaire existe depuis une centaine d'années. Ils m'ont semblé être un choix clair."

"Alors, que s'est-il passé ? Pourquoi vous a-t-elle choisis ? demanda-t-elle.

Il haussa les épaules, "Je pense que Lydia aime Fredrich si nous sommes honnêtes. Ils ont parlé pratiquement tout le temps pendant la réunion, même quand j'avais des questions à lui poser. Honnêtement, j'avais l'impression que je n'étais même pas là. "

Maria sourit, mais avant qu'elle ne puisse dire quoi que ce soit Britta chantait, "Fredrich et Lydia assis dans un arbre, K-I-S-S-S-I-N-G !"

Luca rit et se joignit à elle, Johannes et Maria secouant la tête devant les deux enfants.

Ils ont tous fini leur petit-déjeuner et Maria a regardé l'horloge sur le mur en se rendant compte de l'heure qu'il était.

"Tu ferais mieux de te dépêcher ou tu vas être en retard au travail." Chided Maria, légèrement souriant à lui.

Johannes se tint debout de la table et se dirigea vers l'évier, y plaçant son assiette et sa tasse de café vide avant de retourner à la table où sa famille était assise.
"D'accord, soyez gentils avec maman." Il a dit, embrassant le haut de la tête de Britta, puis celle de Luca.

"Nous le ferons." dit Luca, regardant sa petite sœur pour confirmation, à laquelle elle hocha également la tête, les yeux bleus grands ouverts.

Ils étaient tous les deux des enfants assez bien élevés ; ils avaient juste plus d'énergie qu'ils ne savaient quoi en faire. Heureusement, c'était l'été, donc il y avait beaucoup de plaisir à s'amuser dehors dans la cour arrière, ce qui les fatiguait - courir dans les arroseurs, jouer dans la piscine gonflable pour enfants, jouer au ballon, ou jouer dans le gymnase de la jungle. Ce serait une belle journée pour eux tous, Maria en était sûre. Elle mettait les deux enfants dans leur maillot de bain, puis ils jouaient tous dans la cour arrière sous le soleil chaud.

Il pressa un baiser sur le front de Britta et de Luca avant de se diriger vers la porte pour prendre sa mallette.

Il a revérifié pour s'assurer qu'il avait tout : portefeuille, clés, porte-documents, téléphone. Tout était là où il devait être.

Maria suivit Johannes jusqu'à la porte d'entrée, sortant sur le porche avec lui pour lui souhaiter une bonne journée.

C'était un peu frais pour un matin de juillet, mais elle n'avait pas froid car elle se tenait debout dans son bas de pyjama et un t-shirt léger. Elle savait qu'à midi, il ferait assez chaud pour qu'elle débatte avec ses enfants dans leur piscine gonflable.

"Serez-vous de retour à une heure normale ? À temps pour le dîner, demanda-t-elle en gardant le pied dans la porte pour pouvoir voir Britta et Luca à table en train de manger.

"Pas plus tard que 19h30." Il a promis de l'embrasser pour lui dire au revoir et de se diriger vers sa voiture.

Maria salua Maria en le regardant sortir de l'allée avant qu'elle ne rentre à l'intérieur. Elle a décidé que si Britta et Luca décidaient de faire une sieste en même temps qu'elle chercherait des maisons plus proches de la ville. Elle était consciente que cela pourrait être un peu dur pour Lucas, mais elle était sûre qu'il pourrait se faire de nouveaux amis facilement.

Johannes avait une assez longue route pour se rendre au travail - près d'une heure - et il se retrouvait constamment coincé dans les embouteillages sur le chemin du travail. Il le méprisait, vraiment. C'était la pire partie de son travail, mais heureusement, c'était vraiment la *seule* chose qu'il n'aimait pas dans son travail. Il aimait être avocat et toute l'aide qu'il pouvait offrir aux gens, mais conduire près d'une heure - parfois plus que cela avec la circulation - était incroyablement irritant.

Alors qu'il se dirigeait vers l'autoroute, il pouvait déjà voir les feux de freinage de la majorité des wagons déjà en marche.

Avec un soupir, il a tourné le dos à la radio, la transformant en son émission radiophonique matinale préférée et se préparant à s'asseoir dans un embouteillage.

Au moins, il était bien nourri ce matin. L'autre semaine, il était parti si vite et s'était pratiquement endormi au volant sans sa tasse de café du matin. C'était vraiment un miracle qu'il y soit parvenu.

Johannes s'est concentré sur l'émission-débat - ils discutaient de quelque chose sur la culture pop qui ne semblait pas pouvoir l'intéresser.

Après 15 minutes d'attente dans les embouteillages, son téléphone a commencé à sonner. Il l'a sorti de sa poche et a répondu sans regarder l'identité de l'appelant.

Bien que ce ne fût de toute façon pas nécessaire parce qu'il aurait connu la voix de son petit frère n'importe où.

"Hé, Johan ! Comment allez-vous ? demanda Sebastian.

Johannes a levé les yeux sur la voix enthousiaste de son frère si tôt le matin et a dit : "Je vais bien, Basti. Je ne pensais pas que tu te réveillais si tôt le matin."

Son frère a ri avant de dire : "Ouais, ouais, ouais, ouais, vas-y, fais des blagues, mais j'appelle avec de bonnes nouvelles."

"Vraiment ? Qu'est-ce que c'est alors ? demanda Johannes.

"Gisela et moi allons avoir un bébé !" s'exclama-t-il.

"Oh mon Dieu, Basti, félicitations !" dit Johannes, certainement heureux pour son jeune frère.

Sebastian et Gisela étaient mariés depuis 3 ans et s'étaient rencontrés environ 9 ans auparavant. Ils s'étaient aperçus qu'ils n'avaient presque rien en commun, mais qu'ils s'entendaient à merveille. Elles essayaient d'avoir un bébé depuis un an, mais cela avait été difficile pour elles. Johannes pensait qu'ils avaient abandonné après l'échec de leur dernière tentative.

Apparemment non.

"Où en est Gisi ?" demanda Johannes.

"Deux mois. On voulait s'assurer que tout allait bien avant de commencer à le dire aux gens."

C'était logique pour Johannes. Il savait que s'ils l'avaient dit plus tôt et qu'il se serait passé quelque chose, ils auraient été encore plus déçus d'avoir à le dire aux autres. Il semble, cependant, que 2 mois étaient assez loin pour qu'ils et leur médecin se sentent confiants au sujet de la situation.

"Tu sais, maman va être ravie." Johannes a ri.

Sebastian riait aussi. Les deux hommes savaient que leur mère *adorait les* enfants, ce qui n'était pas surprenant étant donné qu'elle avait été enseignante à la maternelle.

Après la naissance de Britta et de Lucas, elle avait voulu passer chaque instant avec eux. Elle était allée chez eux, plus que Johannes pendant un certain temps avant qu'ils puissent enfin la convaincre qu'il n'y avait rien de mal à leur donner un peu d'espace. Ce n'était pas qu'ils n'appréciaient pas à quel point elle voulait s'impliquer, parce qu'elle était d'une grande aide, mais cela pouvait parfois suffoquer.

"En fait, je pensais lui dire ce week-end au dîner..."

Johannes a levé les yeux et a dit : "C'est une longue pause où je saute pour dire que Maria, les enfants, et moi, je vais venir ?"

"Je savais que je pouvais compter sur toi !" dit Sebastian en riant,"Je t'appellerai samedi matin pour t'en dire plus."

"Tu m'es redevable, Basti." dit Johannes en levant les yeux, même s'il ne pouvait pas garder le sourire de son visage.

"Je paierai un verre au restaurant." Proposa Sebastian.

"Oh non, tu ne t'en sortiras pas si facilement. Tu fais du baby-sitting pour Maria et moi le mois prochain. J'ai des vacances, et on veut une escapade sans les enfants."

"Tu es diabolique." Dit Sebastian, en riant.

"Vous en avez un en route, vous feriez mieux de vous habituer à traiter avec des enfants. Je t'entraîne."

"Très bien. On en parlera au dîner ce week-end."

Sebastian raccrocha alors le téléphone, laissant Johannes rire Johannes pour un moment.

Jusqu'à ce qu'il réalise qu'il était toujours coincé dans les embouteillages

English Translation

The blaring sound of Johannes' alarm clock woke him, much like it did every weekday morning. He worked as a lawyer at a very successful law firm, and he had been there for 9 years. He had worked hard to be where he was now, a partner at the firm.

He suppressed a groan and rolled over, silencing the alarm before rolling back over to kiss his wife good morning. Just because he enjoyed his work did not mean he enjoyed having to wake up at 5:30 in the morning 5 days a week.

"Good morning, Maria."

"Good morning." She mumbled, attempting to shake the sleep from her body.
The two had been married for 10 years and had known each other since kindergarten. They had been practically inseparable since the first day they met, and that had not changed over the years. They truly had married their best friend.

Maria did not technically need to be awake yet, but she knew that their two children would likely be up within the next hour anyway.

"I am going to take a shower." Said Johannes, kissing her forehead before he disappeared into the bathroom.

Maria kicked the blankets from her legs, not bothering to make the bed before she went to the kitchen to start breakfast.

Their daughter, the younger of the two children at age 4 named Britta, was currently going through a phase where the only things she ever wanted to eat were yogurt, chicken nuggets, and eggs. It certainly made breakfast for her easier, though Maria had to admit she was a bit worried that it would continue for an extended period of time. Her daughter could not just survive off chicken nuggets, eggs, and yogurt.

Luca, their 6-year-old son, on the other hand, had practically nothing he *would not* eat. He seemed to be just like Johannes if Maria really thought about it. Both of them would typically eat until they were well past full. She thought it had a lot to do with Luca watching Johannes eat because Maria was certain that he had not learned that from her.

She could not complain, though, because Luca would more than willingly eat whatever Britta was in the mood for. Still, she hoped that her daughter would soon move on to expanding her diet again. There was only so long that she could justify feeding her 3 foods or argue with her about eating her vegetables.

As Maria began preparing breakfast for the rest of the family, Johannes was getting ready for work.

He had finished showering, washing and conditioning his hair, and was now in his work slacks and a blue button-down shirt, his gray tie loose around his neck as he squeezed toothpaste onto his toothbrush and brushed his teeth.

He quickly brushed his hair and pulled on his shoes, socks, and fixed his tie as he headed out of their bedroom and down the hallway into their children's rooms to wake them.

To his surprise, though, neither were still in their beds, but they were still unmade. When he entered the kitchen, he saw why.

Both Britta and Luca were sitting in the high stools that lined the kitchen island as they watched Maria finishing up breakfast. Luca and Britta were quietly talking to each other. It sounded like Luca was telling his younger sister about what school was like. He was going to be starting second grade in August, and it seemed that Britta had a lot of questions about it.

"Are you still going to see your friends?" asked Britta, eyes wide as she looked at her brother.

"Of course." He answered easily, "We are in the same class."

"And they will be for a few years." Added Maria, "It is not until middle school that you might have a few classes without some of them."

Britta's eyes widened as she looked between her older brother and her mother as she asked, "What do you mean? Will you miss them?"

Luca laughed and said, "It is not like I will not see them again. We just have more teachers than just one when we go to the big school."

Maria nodded in agreement and Britta seemed to think over their words carefully before responding.

"So, what do you learn in school, Luca?" she asked.

"A lot of different things. We learn about spelling and writing and math like adding and subtracting and science too." He explained with a smile. It was obvious he was proud of what he had been learning.

"I want to learn to spell too, Mama." She said, looking at Maria expectantly.

Maria chuckled and said, "You already know how to spell your name, Britta. You are learning to spell."

This answer seemed to appease Britta, so she and Luca both turned their attention back to their mother.

Maria had made eggs, bacon, and buttered buns; it all smelled wonderful. Johannes glanced at the clock in the kitchen and realized he only had 15 minutes to eat before he needed to leave. It was a guarantee that he would get stuck in rush hour traffic at 7 in the morning – which he hated. They lived roughly an hour from the law firm, but with the traffic, it sometimes took over an hour and a half.

He and Maria had been talking about moving closer to the city, and he hoped that they would. It was not just that he would be closer to his job, but the schools in the city were better than the countryside where they lived now. It was not necessarily that the schools where they lived were *bad*; they just were not as good as the ones that were closer to the city.

Luca was starting elementary school in August, and Britta would be starting kindergarten in a few years, so Johannes and Maria both wanted them to be at the best schools they could. They were firm believers in education – they had both gone to great schools growing up – so they wanted to give their children the same opportunity.

Moving closer to the city would also allow Johannes to spend more time with the family by not having to leave so early and get home so late. It was typical that by the time he got home at around 20:00, Britta and Luca were both tucked into bed asleep. The only day that Maria allowed them to *try* and stay awake was Friday, but even then, it was unlikely that either of the children would be able to stay awake long enough to see him. Luca had accomplished it two or three times, while Britta had never managed to keep her eyes open past 19:00.

And of course, after a full day of taking care of Luca and Britta, Maria was exhausted. Since it was summer break both children were home, not just Britta, so Maria spent her days doing laundry, teaching them simple things, and playing games with them throughout the day. She loved being able to care for her children, so they did not have to be in daycare, but she could not deny the fact that it was a lot of work.

She always had dinner ready and waiting for him in the microwave, but he often found her asleep, either on the couch if she had intended to wait for him, or in bed, if she already knew how tired she was. He did not blame her one bit. In fact, he knew he was incredibly lucky to have a wife like her who was willing to do so much for the family. He never would have thought he could find a woman like her – but he had. He would be grateful to her forever. Not only had she given him 2 beautiful children, but she worked just as hard as he did, if not *more*. He knew that Britta and Luca were a handful, and she had to handle them 5 days a week, all day, but she never complained about it.

"Well, good morning." He said, ruffling each of his children's hair, "How are my little birds?"

"Good, Papa!" they said in unison, smiling at him before following their mother's instructions to go and sit at the table.

Luca helped Britta into her chair – always the protective and helpful big brother – before sitting down himself.

Johannes helped his wife carry the food out onto the table, spreading it out between the four of them before both parents joined the table to eat as well.

"What do we say to Mama?" Johannes asked his two children.

"Thank you, Mama!" they echoed each other, both smiling.

Maria smiled and put a little bit of everything onto Luca and Britta's plates, cutting their rolls in half and buttering them for them, before setting the plates down in front of each child again.

"Let me fix your plate." Said Johannes, already handing her a filled plate with a smile.

She could not help but smile back and took the food with a thank you.

"Is anything interesting going on at work today?" asked Maria, taking a sip of her coffee.

Johannes shrugged, "Nowhere near as interesting as I am sure it will be here."

Britta clapped her hands together with a smile, but Luca was the one to speak up.

"Nope! Work is boring, Papa."

Johannes chuckled, ruffling his son's hair again before saying, "I actually agree with you there."

"Did Fredrich end up getting that high-profile case you two were after?" asked Maria, taking a bite of her eggs.

Johannes nodded, and after taking a sip of his coffee said, "Yeah, I was actually pretty surprised. The other law firm that wanted the case has been around for about one hundred years. They seemed like the clear choice to me."

"So, what happened? Why did she pick you two?" she asked.

He shrugged, "I think Lydia likes Fredrich if we are honest. They talked practically the entire time during the meeting, even when I had questions for her. It honestly felt like I was not even there.
"

Maria smiled, but before she could say anything Britta was singing, "Fredrich and Lydia sitting in a tree, K-I-S-S-I-N-G!"

Luca laughed and joined her, Johannes and Maria just shaking their heads at the two children.

They all finished their breakfast, and Maria looked at the clock on the wall, noticing how late it was.

"You better hurry or you are going to be late for work." Chided Maria, lightly smirking at him.

Johannes stood from the table and moved over to the sink, putting his plate and empty coffee cup into it before turning back to the table his family sat at.
"Alright, you both be good for Mama." He said, kissing the top of Britta's head, then Luca's.

"We will." Said Luca, looking at his little sister for confirmation, to which she nodded as well, her blue eyes wide.

They were both fairly well-behaved children; they just had more energy than they knew what to do with. Luckily it was summer, so there was plenty of fun to be had outside in the backyard that would tire them out – running through the sprinklers, playing in the inflatable children's pool, playing ball, or playing on the jungle gym. It would be a nice day for all of them, Maria was sure. She would get the two children into their bathing suits, and then they would all play around in the backyard under the warm sun.

He pressed a kiss to both Britta and Luca's foreheads before heading to the door to grab his briefcase.

He double checked to make sure he had everything – wallet, keys, briefcase, phone. Everything was where it should be.

Maria followed Johannes to the front door, stepping out onto the porch with him to wish him a good day.

It was a bit cool for a July morning, but she was not cold as she stood in her pajama bottoms and a light t-shirt. She knew that by noon, it would be hot enough that she would be debating joining her children in their inflatable pool.

"Will you be back at a normal time? In time for dinner?" she asked, keeping her foot in the door so she could still see Britta and Luca at the table eating.

"No later than 19:30." He promised, kissing her goodbye and heading to his car.

Maria waved, watching as he pulled out of the driveway before she went back inside. She decided that if Britta and Luca decided to take a nap at the same time that she would look into houses that were closer to the city. She was aware that it could be a bit hard on Lucas, but she was sure that he would be able to make new friends easily.

Johannes had a fairly long drive to work – close to an hour – and he constantly got stuck in traffic on the way to and from work. He despised it, really. It was the worst part of his job, though luckily it was really the *only* thing he disliked about his job. He enjoyed being a lawyer and all the help he could offer people, but driving close to an hour – sometimes more than that with traffic – was incredibly irritating.

As he moved toward the interstate, he could already see brake lights on the majority of the cars already on.

With a sigh he flipped on the radio, turning it to his favorite morning talk show and preparing to sit in a traffic jam.

At least he was well-fed this morning. Just the other week he had left in such a hurry and had practically been falling asleep at the wheel without his morning cup of coffee. It was truly a miracle that he had made it in at all.

Johannes focused on the talk show – they were discussing something about pop culture that he just could not seem to get interested in.

After 15 minutes of sitting in traffic, his phone began ringing. He dug it out of his pocket and answered without looking at the caller id.

Though it was unnecessary anyway because he would have known his younger brother's voice anywhere.

"Hey, Johan! How are you?" asked Sebastian.

Johannes rolled his eyes at his brother's enthusiastic voice this early in the morning and said, "I'm good, Basti. I did not think you were awake this early in the morning."

His brother laughed before saying, "Yeah, yeah, yeah, go ahead and make jokes, but I am calling with great news."

"Really? What is it then?" asked Johannes.

"Gisela and I are having a baby!" he exclaimed excitedly.

"Oh my god, Basti, congratulations!" said Johannes, certainly happy for his younger brother.

Sebastian and Gisela had been married for 3 years and had met roughly 9 years before. They had found that though they had next to nothing in common, they got along wonderfully. They had been trying to have a baby for the past year, but it had been difficult for them. Johannes thought that they had actually given up after their last attempt had failed.

Apparently not.

"How far along is Gisi?" Johannes asked.

"Two months. We wanted to make sure everything was okay before we started telling people."

It made sense to Johannes. He knew that if they would have told people earlier and something would have happened, they would have been even more heartbroken by having to tell others. It seemed, though, that 2 months was far enough along for them and their doctor to feel confident about the situation.

"You know, Mom is going to be ecstatic." Johannes laughed.

Sebastian laughed as well. Both men knew that their mother absolutely *adored* children, which was no surprise considering she had been a kindergarten teacher.

After the birth of both Britta and Lucas, she had wanted to spend every moment with them. She had been over at their house, more than Johannes had for a while before they were finally able to convince her that it was okay to give them a bit of space. It was not that they did not appreciate how involved she wanted to be, because she was a big help, but it could just feel suffocating at times.

"I was actually thinking about telling her this weekend at dinner..."

Johannes rolled his eyes and said, "Is that long pause where I jump in and say that Maria, the kids, and I will come along?"

"I knew I could count on you!" laughed Sebastian, "I will call you Saturday morning to tell you more."

"You owe me, Basti." Said Johannes, rolling his eyes even though he could not keep the smile from his face.

"I will pay for drinks at the restaurant." Offered Sebastian.

"Oh no, you are not getting off that easy. You are babysitting for Maria and me next month. I have vacation time, and we want a getaway without the children."

"You are evil." Said Sebastian, laughing.

"You have one on the way; you better get used to dealing with children. I am giving you practice."

"Fine. We will talk about it at dinner this weekend."

Sebastian hung up the phone then, leaving Johannes chuckling to himself for a moment.

Until he realized he was still stuck in traffic.

Chapter 6: Going to the Dog Park/ Aller au parc canin

"Tu es presque prête, Katrina?" demanda Joseph de sa place sur le canapé.

"Une seconde!", elle a rappelé, luttant pour se glisser dans ses baskets.

Ils allaient au parc canin avec leur pitbull, Chloé. Elle n'avait que 5 mois, mais elle était déjà une masse musculaire solide, et elle *adorait* jouer. Le parc qu'ils allaient aménager à trois semblait être son préféré sur les trois où ils l'avaient emmenée au cours des derniers mois de sa venue.

Ce parc particulier s'étendait sur plus de trente acres d'espace libre où les chiens pouvaient aller sans être tenus en laisse - c'est probablement pour cette raison que Chloé l'aimait tant. Joseph et Katrina n'avaient pas tout à fait réussi à lui apprendre à marcher en laisse de façon efficace, alors elle s'enchevêtait encore assez souvent dans la laisse, même si elle semblait au moins aller mieux.

"Elle a appelé Joseph d'où elle était, dans leur chambre à coucher, à la recherche de son portefeuille. Il n'était pas rare qu'elle le perde, surtout quand elle était pressée. Elle jura qu'il avait son propre esprit et qu'il agissait de son propre chef, mais elle et Joseph savaient tous les deux que ce n'était pas le cas. Elle était juste douée pour égarer - *perdre* - des choses.

Tous les jours, elle perdait quelque chose, qu'il s'agisse de ses clés, de son portefeuille, de son téléphone, de ses bijoux ou d'une paire de chaussures. S'il pouvait être perdu, il y avait des chances qu'elle le perde à un moment donné.

"Tu veux dire ce portefeuille?" demanda-t-il, apparaissant dans l'entrée de leur chambre, tenant son portefeuille avec un sourire sur son visage.

Après les années qu'ils étaient ensemble, il a commencé à voir qu'il y avait des endroits communs à regarder quand elle disait qu'il lui manquait quelque chose. La cuisine était toujours un bon endroit pour regarder, ainsi que sous la table basse dans le salon, le panier à linge de la salle de bain, et même la boîte aux lettres juste devant leur porte.

Elle avait été accroupi, regardant sous leur lit, alors elle se tint rapidement debout, un regard penaud sur son visage alors qu'elle s'approchait de lui.
"Où était-ce?"

"Dans la cuisine." dit-il en souriant, glissant le petit portefeuille dans sa poche arrière, pressant simultanément un léger baiser sur ses lèvres. "Vous perdriez votre tête si elle n'était pas attachée à votre cou."

Elle a ri de la blague et a accepté. Elle ne sait pas ou ne comprend pas pourquoi, mais elle est heureuse qu'il *ne* soit *pas* comme elle à cet égard. L'un d'eux devait être capable de tout garder ensemble.

"Allez, Chloé est clairement excitée." dit-elle en souriant, montrant où elle faisait les cent pas devant la porte, la queue remuant joyeusement.

Joseph gloussa et lui prit la main, la retira de la chambre et prit la laisse de Chloé dans son autre main. Il a glissé sa main dans la boucle en haut de la laisse avant d'ouvrir la porte d'entrée de leur appartement et de les conduire sur les quelques marches de la rue.

Le parc n'était pas très loin de l'endroit où ils vivaient en métro, et ils avaient souvent pris le métro avec Chloé au cours des dernières semaines, et elle avait bien réussi. Elle était encore un peu nerveuse avec les étrangers, surtout avec tant d'entre eux au même endroit, mais Joseph et Katrina s'étaient rendu compte que tant qu'ils la gardaient entre eux, elle se sentait en sécurité.

Elle n'avait jamais grogné sur qui que ce soit ou agi agressivement, alors même si elle n'avait pas été muselée, ils doutaient tous les deux qu'elle n'aurait jamais agi par agressivité envers qui que ce soit. Elle était bien trop gentille pour ça.

Katrina s'arrêta pour sortir la muselière du sac à dos de Joseph et la mit sur Chloé - comme c'était la règle quand on emmenait de gros animaux dans un wagon plein de gens - avant de descendre dans la station de métro.

Comme Chloé n'était pas une chienne d'assistance, Joseph et Katrina lui ont aussi acheté un billet, les scannant tous les trois alors qu'ils marchaient vers leur plate-forme.

Il n'y avait que 4 arrêts entre l'endroit où ils montaient et celui où ils descendaient, ce qui semblait convenir parfaitement à Chloé. Katrina avait l'impression qu'elle savait où ils allaient et qu'elle pouvait à peine contenir son enthousiasme. Elle était assise calmement, mais sa queue n'arrêtait pas de remuer joyeusement.

L'idée d'avoir un chien venait de Joseph, car Katrina n'avait jamais eu d'animaux domestiques et n'avait pas eu envie d'en avoir maintenant, mais il l'avait convaincue. Cela n'avait pas vraiment été *très* convaincant, mais il était clair que si elle avait vécu seule, elle n'aurait pas eu d'animal de compagnie - même le poisson n'était pas une option.

Ils étaient allés dans un refuge pour animaux, et au moment où Katrina avait vu Chloé, elle était sûre qu'elle rentrait à la maison avec eux. Elle avait été assez petite, complètement brun foncé, sauf son museau, qui était blanc.

Elle avait été gentille et tout excitée quand ils l'avaient sortie du chenil pour jouer dans la petite zone herbeuse derrière le refuge. Joseph savait qu'il aimerait n'importe quel chien, ils ont fini par le ramener à la maison, alors quand Katrina a senti un tel lien avec Chloé, il n'y a même pas pensé à deux fois.

Il avait toujours eu des chiens en grandissant, avec des chats, quelques poissons et même un serpent. Joseph n'était pas étranger aux animaux de compagnie et il aimait beaucoup les avoir. Il croyait fermement que le fait d'avoir des animaux de compagnie rendait la vie meilleure. Il avait toujours été heureux quand il rentrait de l'école avec des chiens et des chats heureux. Les animaux étaient une zone complètement exempte de jugements, et Joseph pensait qu'il était important que tout le monde puisse ressentir ce sentiment.

Katrina était convaincue qu'elle ne trouverait pas de chien avec qui s'entendre parce qu'elle n'avait jamais eu ce lien avec un animal auparavant. Ses parents n'avaient jamais vraiment aimé les animaux de compagnie, et quand elle avait demandé un chien pour Noël, ils avaient clairement fait comprendre que ce n'était pas une option. Elle s'est alors rendu compte que c'était parce que son père était allergique à la plupart des choses, mais que cela n'avait pas vraiment d'importance à long terme. Elle s'était contentée de ne pas avoir d'animaux domestiques.

Joseph savait depuis le début qu'ils finiraient par partir avec un nouveau membre de la famille.

Et maintenant ils étaient là, presque 4 mois plus tard.

Quand le métro s'est arrêté, ils se sont mis en route avec d'autres personnes et sont sortis de la station. Une fois sortis, Katrina a enlevé la muselière de Chloé, qui a secoué son corps dans ce qui semblait être une tentative de se débarrasser du souvenir de l'avoir porté.

Joseph et Katrina ont ri.

Ils ont fait la marche de 10 minutes rapidement, en marchant à travers la grande porte qui séparait le parc du reste de la ville. C'était agréable d'être si immergé dans la nature, tout en restant incroyablement proche de la civilisation - même si on n'en avait pas l'impression une fois que l'on a vraiment commencé à marcher et à explorer le parc.

"Quelle piste devrions-nous faire aujourd'hui, Chloé?" demanda Joseph, en regardant entre elle et Katrina.

Katrina rit et dit: "Voyons où elle veut aller."

Ils marchèrent en avant sur le chemin qu'ils savaient bifurqueraient dans deux directions, et quand c'est arrivé, ils suivirent Chloé vers la droite. Sa queue frémissait d'excitation et son nez semblait collé au sol alors qu'elle essayait d'inhaler toutes les nouvelles odeurs dans le parc.

"C'est plutôt calme ici aujourd'hui." Ils remarquèrent Joseph alors qu'ils s'enfonçaient plus loin dans la vaste étendue d'arbres.

Katrina hocha la tête: "C'est vrai, mais c'est mardi. Ce n'est pas comme s'il était normal que les gens ne travaillent pas."

"Tu as raison, tu as raison." D'accord Joseph, la tirant plus près avec un bras autour de la taille, "Nous avons de la chance de pouvoir travailler de chez nous."

Katrina ne pouvait s'empêcher d'être d'accord avec cela, bien qu'ils aient certainement travaillé dur pour pouvoir le faire. Travailler à domicile - gérer sa propre entreprise - n'était pas facile, et il y avait certainement eu des moments où les deux avaient voulu abandonner.

Ils tenaient une boutique en ligne spécialisée dans la bijouterie artisanale, la menuiserie et la ferronnerie.

Katrina était très douée pour fabriquer des bijoux, qu'il s'agisse de grandes pièces ou de petites et complexes. Ses préférées étaient celles qui contenaient des cristaux ou des pierres précieuses d'une sorte ou d'une autre qu'elle pouvait emballer dans du papier métallique.

Joseph était le menuisier et le monteur de charpentes en bois, comme il l'avait déjà appris de son père avant, il était probablement en sécurité pour lui de le faire. C'était une compétence qu'il avait conservé, travaillant pour plusieurs charpentiers et experts en maçonnerie au cours des années qui ont précédé sa rencontre avec Katrina.

Il n'avait pas fallu longtemps aux deux hommes pour décider que travailler pour d'autres n'était pas du *tout* ce qu'ils voulaient faire de leur vie, alors ils ont commencé à planifier leur entreprise en ligne en vendant des articles faits à la main.

Dans l'ensemble, tout allait très bien, et si leur chance continuait, ils envisageaient d'ouvrir un magasin de briques et de mortier à quelques kilomètres de chez eux.

"Je ne sais pas comment nous avons réussi à rester sains d'esprit avant de pouvoir faire ça." Elle a admis, s'appuyant contre Joseph pendant qu'ils continuaient à laisser Chloé diriger. Ils savaient tous les deux qu'ils arrivaient à l'un des parcs où ils pouvaient laisser Chloé sans laisse - et par la façon dont elle tirait, il semblait qu'elle le savait aussi.

Joseph gloussa et pressa un baiser à son temple avant de dire : "Détermination. Se plaindre."

"Beaucoup de plaintes." Interrompit Katrina avec un sourire.

"Beaucoup de plaintes." Il était d'accord, "Et il savait qu'un jour, nous pourrions le faire si nous continuions d'essayer."

Ils ont percé la clairière pour trouver une zone clôturée avec deux autres chiens et un propriétaire déjà là.

"Bonjour!" salua la femme. Elle était petite et probablement dans la mi-trentaine, avec des cheveux roux vifs qui s'arrêtaient à ses épaules.

"Salut!" dirent Joseph et Katrina, rejoignant la femme à l'intérieur de l'enclos.

"Voici Chloé." Dit Katrina, s'assurant que Chloé était calme avant de la laisser sans laisse.

"Ces deux-là sont Mogli et Kahn." Elle a dit, montrant du doigt le doberman et le lévrier, "Et moi, je suis Cynthia."

"Katrina." Elle dit en souriant: "Et voici Joseph."
"Enchanté de vous rencontrer tous les deux." Elle dit avec un sourire, et Joseph et Katrina répondirent de la même façon.

Cynthia se dirigea vers son sac sur l'un des bancs, laissant Joseph et Katrina regarder Chloé courir et jouer avec Mogli et Kahn.

"Elle aime vraiment être avec d'autres chiens." Dit Joseph, un sourire sournois sur son visage.

Katrina savait exactement où il allait avec cela et a immédiatement dit: "N'y pense même pas, Joseph. Un chien, c'est beaucoup, surtout qu'elle apprend encore."

"Mais regarde comme elle est heureuse là-bas." dit-il en la poussant avec son coude.

"C'est génial, mais ça ne change pas ma réponse. Si vous voulez qu'elle passe plus de temps avec d'autres chiens, vous pouvez l'amener ici plus souvent - ou mieux encore, organisez une sortie avec les chiens de Cynthia ou un de nos amis. Beaucoup d'entre eux ont des chiens qu'elle peut côtoyer."

"Mais..."

"Absolument pas, Joseph." Elle lui dit en le regardant, mais quand elle vit son regard, elle soupira: "Au moins, pas avant l'âge d'un an."

Il sourit, apparemment apaisé quand il lui prit la main et lui pressa un baiser, les jointures, "Je t'aime".

Elle a roulé des yeux mais n'a pas pu garder son sourire de son visage, "Je t'aime aussi."

"Allons jouer avec elle." dit Joseph, glissant le sac à dos qu'il portait sur son dos et retirant quelques jouets de Chloé.

"Chloé!", dit-il en la regardant courir vers eux. Il lui a montré les jouets et lui a lancé une balle.

Katrina et Joseph ont tous les deux regardé Chloé s'envoler comme un coup de feu, poursuivant la balle à travers l'enceinte jusqu'à ce qu'elle l'attrape et commence à courir vers eux avec la balle dans sa bouche.

Ils ont joué à aller chercher avec elle pendant probablement 15 minutes avant qu'elle ne décide qu'elle en avait assez. Ils lui ont donné de l'eau avant de lui remettre sa laisse et de retourner sur le sentier.

Chloé recommençait à tout renifler et à être fascinée par les oiseaux et les écureuils qu'elle pouvait voir du sentier.

"Après quelques minutes de marche tranquille, Katrina demanda à Katrina: " Avez-vous quelque chose à faire aujourd'hui?

Joseph haussa les épaules, prenant sa main dans la sienne avant de dire: " Je crois que oui, mais j'ai un peu de temps pour y arriver. Vraiment?"

Elle secoua la tête: " J'ai fini toutes les commandes jusqu'à jeudi, j'ai donc quelques jours de temps libre. Je peux t'aider avec un peu de la tienne si tu veux. Tu sais que je ne suis pas doué pour la sculpture, mais je me suis certainement amélioré avec la coloration."

Joseph hocha la tête avec un sourire fier: "Tu as eu un grand maître. je n'en attendais pas moins."

Elle s'est cognée son épaule contre la sienne en disant: "Soit tu veux mon aide, soit tu n'en veux pas."

"Tu sais, c'est vrai." Il a dit en riant:"J'ai toujours eu besoin de l'aide d'une belle femme."

A ce moment-là, Chloé a aboyé, comme si elle ne voulait pas être laissée de côté, alors Joseph ajouta: "Une belle femme et son mignon chien".

Katrina rit, et Chloé semblait heureuse. Tous les trois tournent à gauche sur un nouveau chemin qui les ramènera à l'entrée. Ils étaient au parc depuis près de 3 heures à ce moment-là, et il semblait que tout le monde commençait à être un peu fatigué.

Heureusement, il n'était que 14 h, alors ils ont eu tout le temps de se reposer un peu avant de préparer le dîner.

"Tu veux t'arrêter au kebab döner sur le chemin du retour? demanda Joseph en sortant du parc et en retournant dans la rue principale.

"Oh, définitivement! Nous n'y sommes pas allés depuis toujours. Je l'ai raté, c'est sûr." Elle a accepté. "Et toi, Chloé? Qu'est-ce que tu veux pour dîner?"

Joseph a ri et a dit:"Je crois qu'on a encore du poulet que tu lui as fait griller hier."

"Vous voulez dire qu'elle n'a pas tout mangé? C'est une surprise."

Joseph gloussa et avoua: "Je ne lui ai pas tout donné. Sinon, elle l'aurait certainement fait."

"Eh bien, je suppose que c'est réglé! A l'endroit du kebab! s'exclama-t-elle, rebondissant sur ses orteils avec excitation.

Joseph a juste souri en la regardant, lui prenant la main alors qu'ils descendaient la rue pour aller chercher leur nourriture avant de reprendre le métro.

Katrina attendait dehors avec Chloé pendant que Joseph allait chercher leur nourriture - ce qu'ils avaient toujours quand ils venaient ici. Elle s'accroupit devant Chloé et se gratta le dos en riant quand Chloé lui lécha la joue.

"Stupide fille." dit Katrina en souriant.

Quelques minutes plus tard, Joseph sortit avec un grand sac en papier à la main, prenant celui de Katrina avec l'autre et la laissant tenir la laisse pendant qu'ils marchaient vers la station de métro pour rentrer chez eux.

Juste à l'extérieur des marches, Katrina a demandé à Joseph de se retourner pour qu'elle puisse creuser dans le sac à dos avant de remettre le museau de Chloé. Après avoir acheté les trois billets, ils se sont dirigés vers le quai qui les ramènerait à la maison.

"A quoi pensais-tu pour le dîner?" Katrina m'a demandé: "Je vais peut-être devoir aller à l'épicerie si vous voulez quelque chose de substantiel, parce que je ne pense pas qu'il nous reste beaucoup de choses à la maison".

Joseph haussa les épaules, "Nous pouvons aller faire l'épicerie demain. Je suis sûr que nous avons des restes du week-end que nous pouvons manger."

Katrina hocha la tête; un peu soulagée qu'elle n'ait pas à s'aventurer à nouveau hors de la maison aujourd'hui. Elle ne s'en était pas rendu compte lorsqu'ils étaient au parc, mais son corps était épuisé par les activités de la matinée.

Le métro s'est arrêté quelques minutes plus tard, et les trois sont montés à bord, montant les 4 arrêts jusqu'à leur propre arrêt. Comme lorsqu'ils sont arrivés, le métro n'était pas plein, la plupart d'entre eux revenaient déjà du déjeuner et attendaient de rentrer chez eux après le travail pour faire la navette.

Une fois sortis de la station de métro, Katrina a enlevé la muselière de Chloé et l'a remise dans le sac à dos de Joseph avant qu'ils ne rentrent tous les trois à pied à leur appartement.

C'était un peu un soulagement de rentrer chez eux, malgré le plaisir qu'ils avaient eu ce jour-là. Même Chloé semblait épuisée, s'allongeant immédiatement sur le plancher de bois franc frais du salon.

Joseph et Katrina s'asseyaient autour de la table basse dans le salon, allumant la télévision et retirant leur déjeuner.

"Ça sent aussi bon que d'habitude." dit Katrina, en ouvrant le récipient en polystyrène qui contenait sa nourriture.

Joseph hocha la tête mais ne dit rien, une bouchée de son kebab déjà dans la bouche.

Chloé, sentant la nourriture, s'assit au bout de la table, attendant de toute évidence une petite gâterie.

Joseph soupira, mais se rendit, lui jetant un petit morceau. Elle avait sa nourriture sèche dans le bol, et il réchauffait son poulet d'hier après qu'il avait fini de manger.

"Tu as passé une bonne journée au parc?" demanda Katrina à Chloé, se grattant derrière l'oreille pendant qu'elle le faisait.

"Je sais que je l'ai fait."

English Translation

"Are you almost ready, Katrina?" asked Joseph from his spot on the couch.

"Just a second!" she called back, struggling to slip into her sneakers.

They were going down to the dog park together with their pit bull, Chloe. She was only 5 months old, but she was already a solid mass of muscle, and she *loved* to play. The park that the three of them were going to seemed to be her favorite out of the 3 they had taken her to over the past few months of having her.

This particular park was over thirty acres of free space where dogs could go without being on leashes – which was probably why Chloe liked it so much. Joseph and Katrina had not quite managed to teach her how to walk on a leash effectively, so she still got tangled in the leash quite often, though she at least seemed to be getting better.

"Okay, let me just grab my wallet, and then I'll be right out!" she called to Joseph from where she was, in their bedroom looking for her wallet. It was not uncommon for her to misplace it, particularly when she was in a hurry. She swore it had a mind of its own and moved on its own accord, but she and Joseph both knew that was not the case. She was just great at misplacing – *losing* – things.

It was practically an everyday occurrence that she would lose something, whether it was her keys, her wallet, her phone, jewelry, or a pair of shoes. If it was able to be lost, chances were that she would lose it at some point.

"You mean this wallet?" he asked, appearing in the doorway to their bedroom holding her wallet with a smirk on his face.

After the years that they had been together, he began to see that there were common locations to look when she said she was missing something. The kitchen was always a good place to look, as well as under the coffee table in the living room, the bathroom clothing hamper, and even the mailbox right outside their door.

She had been crouched down looking under their bed, so she quickly stood, a sheepish look on her face as she approached him. "Where was it?"

"In the kitchen." He said with a smile, slipping the small wallet into her back pocket, simultaneously pressing a light kiss to her lips. "You would lose your head if it was not attached to your neck."

She laughed at the joke and agreed. She did not know or understand why that was the case, but she was glad he was *not* like her in that regard. One of them had to be able to keep everything together.

"Come on, Chloe is clearly excited." She said with a smile, pointing to where she was pacing back and forth in front of the door, her tail wagging happily.

Joseph chuckled and took her hand, pulling her from the bedroom and taking Chloe's leash in his other hand. He slipped his hand through the loop at the top of the leash before opening the front door of their apartment and leading them down the few steps to the street.

The park was not too far from where they lived by subway, and they had often taken the subway with Chloe over the past few weeks, and she had done well. She still got a bit nervous around strangers, especially so many of them in one place, but Joseph and Katrina had realized that as long as they kept her between them, she felt safe.

She had never growled at anyone or acted aggressively, so even if she had not been muzzled, they both doubted that she ever would have acted out of aggression toward anyone. She was far too sweet of a dog for that.

The three of them walked the short distance to the subway station, Katrina stopping to get the muzzle out of Joseph's backpack and put it on Chloe – as were the rules when taking big animals onto a train car full of people – before they continued down into the subway station.

Since Chloe was not a service dog, Joseph and Katrina bought her a ticket as well, scanning all three as they walked toward their platform.

There were only 4 stops between where they got on and where they would be getting off, which seemed to suit Chloe just fine. It seemed to Katrina that she knew where they were headed and could hardly contain her excitement. She was sitting calmly, but her tail never stopped wagging happily.

The idea to get a dog had come from Joseph, as Katrina had never had pets growing up and had not been partial to having any now, but he had convinced her. It had not really taken *that* much convincing, but it was clear that had she been living alone she would not have gotten a pet of any kind – even fish was not an option.

They had gone to an animal rescue shelter, and the moment Katrina had seen Chloe, she was sure that she was coming home with them. She had been fairly small, completely dark brown except her muzzle, which was white.

She had been sweet and nothing but excited when they had taken her out of the kennel to play in the small grassy area behind the shelter. Joseph had known he would love any dog, they ended up taking home, so when Katrina felt such a connection to Chloe, he did not even think twice.

He had always had dogs growing up, along with with with cats, a few fish, and even a snake. Joseph was no stranger to pets and enjoyed having them immensely. He was a firm believer in the fact that having pets made life better. He had always been happy when he came home from school to happy dogs and cats. Animals were a completely judgment-free zone, and Joseph thought it important that everyone got to experience that feeling.

Katrina had been convinced that she would not find a dog that she could get along with because she had never had that connection with an animal before. Her parents had never really liked pets, and when she had asked for a dog one Christmas, they had made it clear that it was *not* an option. She now realized that it was because her father was allergic to most things, but it hadn't really mattered in the long run. She had been content without pets.

Joseph had known from the beginning that they would end up leaving with a new addition to the family, though.

And now here they were, almost 4 months later.

When the subway came to their stop, they shuffled off with a few other people and made their way out of the station. Once they were out, Katrina took the muzzle off Chloe, who shook her body in what seemed like an attempt at ridding herself of the memory of wearing it.

Joseph and Katrina just laughed.

They made the 10-minute walk quickly, walking through the large gate that separated the park from the rest of the town. It was nice to be so immersed in nature, yet still incredibly close to civilization – even if it did not feel like it once you really started walking and exploring the park.

"What trail should we do today, Chloe?" asked Joseph, looking between her and Katrina.

Katrina laughed and said, "Let us see where she wants to go."

They walked forward on the path they knew would branch off in two directions, and when it did, they followed Chloe to the right. Her tail was wagging excitedly, and her nose seemed glued to the ground as she tried to inhale all of the new scents in the park.

"It is pretty quiet here today." Noticed Joseph as they walked further into the vast expanse of trees.

Katrina nodded, "True, but it is Tuesday. It is not like it is normal for people to not be working."

"Right you are." Agreed Joseph, pulling her closer with an arm around her waist, "We are lucky that we get to work from home."

Katrina could not help but agree with that, though they had certainly worked hard to be able to do so. Working from home – running your own business – was not easy, and there had certainly been times when both of them had wanted to give up.

They ran an online shop that specialized in handcrafted jewelry, woodworks, and ironwork.

Katrina was great at making jewelry, whether they be large pieces or small and intricate. Her favorite were ones that contained crystals or gems of some sort that she could wire-wrap.

Joseph was the wood and ironworker, as he had been learning from his dad since before it was probably safe for him to do so. It was a skill that he had stuck with, working for several carpenters and masonry experts over the years before he met Katrina.

It had not taken the two long to decide that working for others was not what they wanted to do with their lives – *at all* – so they began planning for their online business selling handcrafted items.

All in all, everything was going very well, and if their good fortune continued, they were thinking of opening a brick and mortar store a few miles from where they lived.

"I do not know how we managed to stay sane before we were able to do this." She admitted, leaning against Joseph as they continued letting Chloe lead. They both knew they were coming up to one of the playpens where they could let Chloe off of her leash – and by how she was pulling, it seemed she knew it as well.

Joseph chuckled and pressed a kiss to her temple before saying, "Determination. Complaining."

"Lots of complaining." Interrupted Katrina with a smile.

"Lots of complaining." He agreed, "And just the knowledge that one day we would be able to do this if we just kept trying."

They broke through the clearing to find a fenced-in area with two other dogs and one owner already there.

"Hello!" greeted the woman. She was short and probably in her mid-fifties with bright red hair that stopped at her shoulders.

"Hi!" both Joseph and Katrina said, joining the woman inside the pen.

"This is Chloe." Said Katrina, making sure Chloe was calm before letting her off the leash.

"Those two are Mogli and Kahn." She said, pointing to the Doberman and greyhound, "And I'm Cynthia."

"Katrina." She said with a smile, "And this is Joseph."
"It is nice to meet you both." She said with a smile, and Joseph and Katrina responded in kind.

Cynthia headed over to her bag on one of the benches, leaving Joseph and Katrina to watch Chloe run around and play with Mogli and Kahn.

"She really likes being around other dogs." Said Joseph, a sly smile on his face.

Katrina knew exactly where he was going with that and immediately said, "Do not even think about it, Joseph. One dog is plenty, especially since she is still learning."

"But look at how happy she is over there." He said, nudging her with his elbow.

"That is great, but it does not change my answer. If you want her to spend more time with other dogs, then you are welcome to bring her here more often – or better yet, set up a playdate with Cynthia's dogs or one of our friends. Plenty of them have dogs that she can be around."

"But - "

"Absolutely not, Joseph." She said, glaring at him, but when she saw the look on his face, she sighed, "At least not until she is 1."

He smiled, seemingly placated as he took her hand and pressed a kiss to her, knuckles, "I love you."

She rolled her eyes but could not keep her smile from her face, "I love you too."

"Let us go play with her." Said Joseph, sliding the backpack he had been carrying off his back and taking out a few of Chloe's toys.

"Chloe!" he called, watching as she ran toward them. He showed her the toys and then threw one of the balls.

Katrina and Joseph both watched as Chloe took off like a shot, chasing the ball across the enclosure until she caught it and started running back towards them with the ball in her mouth.

They played fetch with her for probably 15 minutes before she decided she had had enough. They gave her some water before putting her leash back on and heading back to the trail.

Chloe was back to sniffing everything and being fascinated by the birds and squirrels she could see from the trail.

"Do you have anything to work on today?" asked Katrina after a few minutes of quiet walking.

Joseph shrugged, taking her hand in his before saying, "I think I do, but I have a while to get it done. Do you?"

She shook her head, "I finished all the orders up until Thursday, so I have a few days of free time. I could help you with some of yours if you want. You know I am no good at the actual carving, but I have certainly gotten better with staining."

Joseph nodded with a proud smile, "You had a great teacher. I would expect no less."

She playfully bumped into his shoulder with her own as she said, "You either want my help, or you do not."

"You know, I do." He said chuckling, "I could always use the help of a beautiful woman."
Just then, Chloe barked, as though she did not want to be left out, so Joseph added, "A beautiful woman and her cute dog."

Katrina laughed, and Chloe seemed pleased. The three of them to a left turn onto a new path that would lead them back to the entrance. They had been at the park for nearly 3 hours at this point, and it seemed that everyone was getting a bit tired.

Luckily it was only 14:00, so they had plenty of time to rest for a bit before making dinner.

"Do you want to stop at that döner kebab place on the way home?" asked Joseph as they made their way out of the park and back onto the main street.

"Oh, definitely! We have not been there in forever. I have missed it for sure." She agreed. "What about you, Chloe? What would you like for dinner?"

Joseph laughed and said, "I think we still have some of that chicken you grilled for her yesterday."

"You mean she did not eat all of it? That is a surprise."

Joseph chuckled and admitted, "I did not give it all to her. Otherwise, she definitely would have."

"Well, I guess that settles it! To the kebab place!" she exclaimed, bouncing on her toes with excitement.

Joseph just smiled as he looked at her, taking her hand as they made their way down the street to pick up their food before getting back on the subway.

Katrina waited outside with Chloe while Joseph went in to get their food – what they always got when they came here. She crouched down in front of Chloe and scratched her back, laughing when Chloe licked her cheek.

"Silly girl." Said Katrina with a smile on her face.

A few minutes later Joseph came out with a large paper bag in his hand, taking Katrina's with the other and letting her keep hold of the leash as they walked toward the subway station to head home.

Just outside the steps, Katrina had Joseph turn around so she could dig through the backpack before putting Chloe's muzzle back on. After purchasing the three tickets, they made their way to the platform that would take them home.

"What were you thinking for dinner?" Katrina asked, "I might need to go to the grocery store if you want something substantial because I do not think we have much left at home."

Joseph shrugged, "We can go grocery shopping tomorrow. I am sure we have leftovers from the weekend that we can eat."

Katrina nodded; a bit relieved that she would not have to venture out of the house again today. She had not realized it while they were at the park, but her body was exhausted from the morning's activities.

The subway pulled up a few minutes later, and the 3 of them got on, riding the 4 stops back to their own stop. Much like when they had first gotten on, the subway was not that full, most already back from lunch and waiting to commute back home after work.

Once they were once again out of the subway station, Katrina removed Chloe's muzzle, putting it back into Joseph's backpack before the three of them made the short walk back to their apartment.

It was a bit of a relief to get home, regardless of the fun they had had that day. Even Chloe seemed exhausted, immediately laying down on the cool hardwood floor of the living room.

Joseph and Katrina sat around the coffee table in the living room, flipping on the TV and pulling out their lunch.

"It smells as good as always." Said Katrina, opening the Styrofoam container that held her food.

Joseph nodded but said nothing, a bite of his kebab already in his mouth.

Chloe, smelling the food, sat at the end of the table, obviously waiting for a little treat.

Joseph sighed but gave in, tossing her a small piece. She had her dry food in the bowl, and he would warm up her chicken from yesterday after he had finished eating.

"Did you have a good day at the park?" Katrina asked Chloe, scratching behind her ear as she did so.

"I know I did."

Chapter 7: Having a Dinner Party/ Organisation d'un dîner

La préparation d'un dîner était toujours mouvementée. Il y avait tellement de choses à prévoir que Kara s'est presque demandé si tout cela en valait la peine.

Elle devait encore cuisiner et ajouter la touche finale à la table pour que tout soit parfait - et il *fallait que* ce *soit* parfait.

Son frère, Lucas, revenait de son année d'études à l'étranger en Australie, et elle était plus que ravie de le revoir. Ils étaient jumeaux et avaient toujours été proches. Ils avaient même vécu ensemble dans un appartement pendant 3 ans avant que Lucas ne décide de saisir l'opportunité d'étudier en Australie.

Mia était heureuse pour lui et l'a certainement encouragé à saisir l'occasion, mais ce serait mentir que de dire qu'il ne lui avait pas beaucoup manqué. C'était étrange de vivre seule après avoir eu sa présence constante dans les parages.

Et maintenant, elle ne savait même pas s'il allait revenir vivre avec elle ou s'il avait d'autres projets. Ils n'en avaient pas vraiment parlé depuis qu'il était parti. Elle ressentait juste une pléthore d'émotions et trouvait difficile de les résoudre toutes.

Sans parler de l'organisation d'un dîner auquel six de leurs amis assisteraient - avec son petit ami et la petite amie de son frère - de sorte qu'il y aurait au total 10 personnes dans son appartement assez petit.

Et elle avait *beaucoup trop* à faire. Décidant qu'elle n'y arriverait pas toute seule, elle a décroché son téléphone et a appelé son petit ami.

"Hé, Mia, qu'est-ce qui se passe?" a-t-il demandé.

"Je *flippe*, Jonathan." dit-elle, faisant les cent pas dans sa cuisine. "Il y a tant à faire, et il n'y a absolument aucune chance que je puisse le faire tout seul!"

Son rire était un peu réconfortant quand il a dit: "Je serai là dans 15 minutes, et nous trouverons la solution ensemble."

"Merci infiniment. Je t'aime! s'exclama-t-elle.

"Je t'aime aussi, mon petit oiseau", dit-il, rassemblant déjà ses affaires pour pouvoir marcher pendant 10 minutes jusqu'à son appartement.

Une fois qu'ils avaient raccroché, Mia s'est sentie un peu plus calme et a décidé de commencer à dîner. Elle avait déjà pané le schnitzel, alors il attendait dans le réfrigérateur pour être cuit, alors elle a commencé à hacher quelques poivrons rouges et oranges.

Quand elle les avait mis dans un bol et rincé la planche à découper, on a frappé à sa porte.

"Entre!" cria-t-elle, sachant que c'était Jonathan - et qu'il avait déjà une clé de toute façon.

Quelques secondes plus tard, Jonathan était dans la cuisine avec elle, l'embrassant en la saluant avant de regarder autour de la cuisine.

"Comment est-ce que c'est déjà le bordel ici?", se moque-t-il.

Elle étouffa un soupir d'indignation en disant: "Tu sais que je n'ai jamais cuisiné pour autant de gens auparavant. Je ne savais même pas ce que j'allais faire jusqu'à il y a une heure, donc la plupart de tout ça n'est pas vraiment pour ce repas."

Il ne pouvait s'empêcher de rire d'elle. Il la trouvait vraiment adorable, surtout quand elle était agitée.

"D'accord, première étape: débarrassons-nous de tout ce que nous n'allons pas utiliser pour préparer ce dîner. Ce sera beaucoup moins accablant comme ça."

Mia acquiesça d'un signe de tête.

"Brocoli?", demanda-t-il en le tenant en l'air.

Elle a secoué la tête et il l'a mise au frigo.

"Pâtes?"

Elle a encore secoué la tête, alors dans le frigo, il est parti.

"Riz?"

"Tu crois qu'on devrait faire du riz avec l'escalope?" demanda-t-elle, apparemment incertaine.

Jonathan acquiesça d'un signe de tête: "Oui, on va laisser tomber."

Après avoir nettoyé les ingrédients inutiles du comptoir, il a sorti une casserole pour le riz. Mia a sorti l'escalope du frigo et a demandé une casserole à Jonathan.

"Combien de temps nous reste-t-il avant que tout le monde commence à venir?" demanda Jonathan, en commençant par le riz.

Mia regarda l'horloge et s'étonna de l'heure à laquelle il était déjà tard.

"Un peu moins d'une heure! Je dois aller chercher le vin que j'ai oublié, et je dois encore préparer les ballons"Welcome Home". Tu crois que tu as la nourriture sous contrôle?"

Jonathan hocha la tête et, souriant, dit: "Allez-y. Je suis une meilleure cuisinière que toi de toute façon."

Elle ne voulait pas l'admettre, mais elle savait qu'il avait raison. Elle était douée pour cuisiner, mais il était presque chef.

Au lieu d'essayer de nier l'évidence, elle a pris son sac à main et ses clés sur la table près de la porte et est allée chercher du vin à l'épicerie la plus proche. Heureusement, elle ne vivait qu'à 5 minutes d'une épicerie, donc elle savait que cela ne lui prendrait pas trop de temps.

Il faisait beau dehors. Il faisait chaud avec une brise fraîche qui froissait légèrement ses cheveux, et pour l'instant, le ciel était bleu et sans nuages. Elle aurait pu jurer que la météo annonçait qu'il allait pleuvoir.

Elle se dépêchait d'aller vite au cas où il allait pleuvoir. La dernière chose dont elle avait besoin, c'était de se faire prendre par le mauvais temps. Elle était déjà habillée, son maquillage était fini, ses cheveux étaient coiffés, et elle n'aurait jamais eu le temps de réparer quoi que ce soit si cela se gâtait maintenant.

Arrivée au magasin un peu plus de 5 minutes plus tard, elle s'est rendue directement à l'allée des vins. Elle a ramassé du vin rouge et du vin blanc et les a payés à la caisse.

Lorsqu'elle est rentrée chez elle un peu moins de 20 minutes plus tard, Jonathan était encore dans la cuisine.

"Avez-vous trouvé ce que vous cherchiez?"
Mia hocha la tête: "Oui, les voilà." dit-elle, agitant le sac avec les bouteilles de vin.

"Mettez-les dans le frigo et installez-le dans le salon. J'ai la cuisine sous contrôle." Dit Jonathan, pressant un baiser sur son front alors qu'elle passait devant lui.

"Je t'ai dit que je t'aimais dernièrement?" demanda-t-elle avec un sourire.

Il gloussa, "Tu l'as peut-être dit une ou deux fois."

Alors qu'elle se rendait dans le salon pour installer les ballons et les banderoles et mettre la table, Jonathan restait dans la cuisine pours continuer à faire cuire les aliments.

Elle avait acheté des ballons qui s'écrivaient'Welcome Home Lucas', alors elle a commencé par ceux-là. Après avoir remis les ballons en ordre, elle s'est dirigée vers les banderoles, puis est retournée dans la cuisine pour sortir les assiettes et l'argenterie pour la table.

Elle avait placé une nappe blanche sur la table en bois brun foncé plus tôt, alors elle s'est rapidement mise au travail, mettant les dix assiettes autour de la table avec les couteaux et les fourchettes.

Alors qu'elle aidait Jonathan à apporter la nourriture à table, on a frappé à la porte. Tous les deux pouvaient entendre leurs amis à l'extérieur de la porte. Mia leur avait dit de venir devant Lucas pour qu'ils puissent tous être là pour le surprendre.

Il n'avait aucune idée que cette fête avait lieu, et Mia voulait que ce soit parfait.

"Elle a appelé de la salle à manger alors qu'elle et Jonathan prenaient dix verres de vin pour mettre sur la table.

Leurs 6 amis - Julia, Michael, Kevin, Laura, Vivian et Susanna - sont passés par la porte et ont accueilli Mia et Jonathan avec des câlins.

"À quelle heure sera-t-il là? demanda Michael en prenant les vestes de tout le monde et en les accrochant dans le placard du couloir.

"Il m'a envoyé un texto il y a quelques minutes disant qu'il venait d'aller chercher Thea, donc ils devraient être là dans 5 minutes." Dit Mia, rebondissant pratiquement dans son excitation.

"Très bien, tout le monde à table, puis j'ouvrirai la porte et prétendrai que tout est normal, puis on entrera dans la salle à manger, et vous crierez tous surprise." J'ai dit à Mia.

Tout le monde hocha la tête et s'assit à table. L'enthousiasme de tout le monde dans la salle était presque palpable. Personne ne parlait au cas où Lucas pourrait les entendre de l'extérieur.

Peu de temps après, on a frappé à la porte, et Mia n'a pas pu s'empêcher de voir le sourire géant qui se répandait sur son visage alors qu'elle allait ouvrir la porte.

Elle a ouvert la porte et a vu son frère et Thea. Avant qu'elle n'ait le temps de faire quoi que ce soit, Lucas l'a prise dans ses bras.

"Tu m'as tellement manqué, soeurette." Il chuchota en la serrant fort dans ses bras.

Elle le serra tout aussi fort dans ses bras et lui répondit: "Tu m'as manqué aussi. Je suis si contente que tu sois rentré."

Une fois qu'ils ont cessé de serrer Mia dans leurs bras, Mia a également serré Thea dans ses bras et les a fait entrer tous les deux à l'intérieur.

Lucas vit les ballons que Mia avait mis en place et sourit, mettant son bras autour de ses épaules en disant: "Tu n'avais pas besoin de faire ça".

"Je sais." Elle répondit avec un petit sourire et dit: "Viens. J'ai préparé le dîner."

"Vous avez cuisiné aussi?" demanda Lucas avec un petit rire, en la suivant dans la salle à manger.

"Surprise!" cria tout le monde.

Les yeux de Lucas s'élargirent en état de choc, mais il eut bientôt un sourire géant sur son visage.

"Vous n'aviez vraiment pas à vous donner tout ce mal." dit-il, toujours souriant.

Susanna haussa les épaules, "Nous venons d'arriver. Jonathan et Mia sont ceux qui ont fait tout le vrai travail."

Tout le monde acquiesça d'un signe de tête et Lucas embrassa Jonathan pour le remercier avant de se retourner vers sa sœur.

"Bienvenue à la maison." dit-elle doucement, un petit sourire sur son visage.

Il l'a encore serrée dans ses bras et lui a dit:"Tu as vraiment fait mon plat préféré aussi ?"

Elle acquiesça d'un signe de tête: "C'est une fête pour toi. Bien sûr, j'ai fait ton plat préféré."

Une fois que tout le monde s'était installé à table et que la nourriture avait été servie, tout le monde avait un million de questions pour Lucas et le temps qu'il avait passé en Australie.

"Tu as vu des kangourous?" demanda Kevin.

Lucas hocha la tête: "Oui, nous avons fait un safari la deuxième semaine où j'étais là-bas, et nous avons pu voir toutes sortes d'animaux - kangourous, lions, éléphants, zèbres - ce fut l'une des expériences les plus cool de ma vie".

"As-tu aimé tes cours?" demanda Vivian. Elle était le petit rat de bibliothèque silencieux du groupe, alors personne n'a été surpris que ce soit sa question.

"Oui, la plupart d'entre eux. Il y a eu une classe pendant les deux semestres que je n'ai pas aimée, mais je pense que la plus grande partie de cela avait plus à voir avec le professeur qu'avec la matière."

"Qu'est-ce qui n'allait pas avec le professeur?" demanda Vivian avec un sourcil levé.

"Il était tellement ennuyeux. J'avais l'impression que ses cours ne finiraient jamais. D'ailleurs, il est difficile de vouloir se concentrer sur la chimie quand on est entouré par la nature sauvage australienne." dit-il en regardant autour de la table ses amis.

"Je ne sais pas comment tu as réussi à camper là-bas pour le cours d'été." Elle a fait trembler Susanna. De tous, elle était la plus jeune fille de toutes, et elle ne pouvait pas s'imaginer devoir passer plus d'un week-end en camping - oubliez tout un été.

Tout le monde autour de la table a ri et Lucas a dit:"Tout le monde ne déteste pas le plein air, Suzy."

"Je ne *déteste pas le* plein air." Susanna a défendu.

"Tu détestes être à l'extérieur." J'ai plaisanté, Mia.

Susanna n'a rien dit d'autre que d'essayer - et d'échouer - de garder le sourire de son visage. Elle savait que ses amis avaient raison. Ils la connaissaient bien.

"Veux-tu y retourner?" demanda Michael.

Lucas haussa les épaules, "Seulement si je pouvais tous vous emmener avec moi, ou si je n'avais pas à être là une année entière sans vous voir."

"Oh, les gars, je crois qu'on lui a manqué." Elle a taquiné Mia, un sourire sur son visage qui correspondait à tous les autres autour de la table.

"Ouais, ouais" dit Lucas en secouant la tête alors qu'il souriait encore.

"Je propose un toast." Dit Mia, en soulevant son verre de vin à moitié rempli. Elle a attendu que les autres fassent de même avant de continuer: "Un toast à mon frère, pour poursuivre ses rêves et les réaliser, même s'il était à des milliers de kilomètres de tous ceux qu'il connaissait. Nous sommes tous très fiers de toi."

"Santé!" a dit tout le monde, en cognant leurs verres ensemble avant de prendre un verre.

"Maintenant je pense qu'il ne reste plus qu'une seule surprise." Dit Lucas, prenant la main de sa soeur alors qu'il la tirait pour se tenir debout sur la table.

Elle le regarda d'un sourcil, confuse en lui demandant: "De quoi parles-tu ? Il n'y a pas d'autres surprises..."

"Si, il y en a une, Mia." dit Lucas, la tournant vers Jonathan, qui était maintenant à genoux devant elle.

"Oh mon Dieu, Jonathan, qu'est-ce que tu fais?" sursauta Mia, sa main allant à sa bouche.

"Je voulais faire ça depuis un moment, mais je savais que c'était un moment où tu voudrais que ton frère soit là, et bien sûr il le voulait aussi." dit Jonathan, prenant la main de Mia dans la sienne tout en tirant une petite boîte de velours noir de sa poche.

"Je t'aime, Mia Safran, et je ne me vois passer le reste de ma vie qu'avec toi. Veux-tu me faire l'honneur de m'épouser?"

"Bien sûr !" s'exclama-t-elle, avec un beau sourire sur le visage,"J'adorerais t'épouser, Jonathan."

Tous les autres applaudissaient, applaudissaient et sifflaient tandis que Jonathan glissait l'anneau sur son doigt et l'embrassait.

Mia n'avait pas pensé que cette journée pouvait se dérouler aussi bien qu'elle l'avait fait, mais elle était heureuse. Non seulement son frère était à la maison, mais elle était fiancée.

Quelle journée!

English Translation

Preparing for a dinner party was always hectic. There was so much that went into planning one that Kara almost wondered if all this was worth it.

She still had to cook and add the finishing touches to the table in order for everything to be perfect – and it *had to be* perfect.

Her brother, Lucas, was coming home from his year studying abroad in Australia, and she was beyond excited to see him again. They were twins and had always been close. They had even lived in an apartment together for 3 years before Lucas had decided to take the opportunity to study in Australia.

Mia had been happy for him and certainly encouraged him to take the opportunity, but it would be a lie to say she had not missed him a lot. It had been strange living by herself after having had his constant presence around.

And now she did not even know if he was going to move back in with her or if he had other plans. They had not really talked about it while he had been away. She was just feeling a plethora of emotions and was finding it difficult to sort them all out.

Let alone to set up an entire dinner party that 6 of their friends would be attending – along with her boyfriend and her brother's girlfriend – so there would be a total of 10 people in her fairly small apartment.

And she had *way too much* to do. Deciding that there was no way she was going to get this done on her own, she picked up her phone and called her boyfriend.

"Hey, Mia, what is going on?" he asked.

"I am *freaking out*, Jonathan." She said, pacing back and forth in her kitchen. "There is so much to do, and there is absolutely no way I am going to be able to get this done by myself!"

His chuckle was slightly comforting as he said, "I will be there in 15 minutes, and we will figure it out together."

"Thank you so much. I love you!" she exclaimed.

"I love you too, birdy," he said, already gathering his things so he could walk the 10 minutes to her apartment.

Once they had hung up, Mia felt a little calmer and decided to start on dinner. She had already breaded the schnitzel, so it was waiting in the fridge to be cooked, so she started chopping a few red and orange peppers.

When she had put them in a bowl and rinsed the cutting board, there was a knock on her door.

"Come in!" she shouted, knowing it was Jonathan – and he already had a key anyway.

A few seconds later, Jonathan was in the kitchen with her, kissing her in greeting before looking around the kitchen.

"How is it already a mess in here?" he teased.

She stifled an indignant sigh as she said, "You know that I have never cooked for this many people before. I did not know what I was even going to make until like an hour ago, so most of this is not actually for this meal."

He could not help but chuckle at her. He found her truly adorable, especially when she was flustered.

"Okay, step one: let us get rid of anything that we are not going to use to make this dinner. It will be way less overwhelming that way."

Mia nodded in agreement.

"Broccoli?" he asked, holding it up.

She shook her head, and he put it in the fridge.

"Pasta?"

She shook her head again, so into the fridge, it went.

"Rice?"

"Do you think we should do rice with the schnitzel?" she asked, seemingly unsure.

Jonathan nodded, "Yeah, we will leave it out."

After cleaning up the unneeded ingredients from the counter, he got out a pot for the rice. Mia got the schnitzel out of the fridge and asked Jonathan for a pan.

"How much time do we have before everyone starts coming over?" asked Jonathan, starting on the rice.

Mia looked at the clock and gasped at how late it had already gotten.

"A little less than an hour! I need to go pick up the wine that I forgot, and I still have to set up the 'Welcome Home' balloons. Do you think you have got the food under control?"

Jonathan nodded and with a smile, said, "Go ahead. I am a better cook than you anyway."

She did not want to admit it, but she knew he was right. She was okay at cooking, but he was practically a chef.

Instead of trying to deny the obvious, she grabbed her purse and keys from the table by the door and headed out to pick up wine from the nearest grocery store. Luckily she only lived 5 minutes from a grocery store, so she knew it would not take her too long.

The weather outside was nice. It was warm with a cool breeze that lightly ruffled her hair, and for now, the skies were blue and free of clouds. She could have sworn that the weather forecast had said it was going to rain.

She hurried her pace just in case it was going to rain. The last thing she needed was to get caught in bad weather. She was already dressed, her makeup was done, her hair was done, and there was no way she would have time to fix any of that if it got ruined now.

Once she arrived at the store a little over 5 minutes later, she went directly to the wine aisle. She picked up red wine and white wine and paid for them at the register.

When she made it back to her apartment a little less than 20 minutes later, Jonathan was still in the kitchen.

"Did you find what you were looking for?"
Mia nodded, "Yep, here they are." She said, waving the bag with the wine bottles.

"Well put those in the fridge and then set up the living room for him. I have the kitchen under control." Said Jonathan, pressing a kiss to her forehead as she walked past him.

"Have I told you that I love you lately?" she asked with a smile.

He chuckled, "You may have said it once or twice."

As she went into the living room to set up the balloons and streamers and to set the dinner table, Jonathan remained in the kitchen continuing to cook the food.

She had bought balloons that spelled out 'Welcome Home Lucas' so she began with those first. After she got the balloons in order, she moved on to the streamers, and then went back into the kitchen to get out the plates and silverware for the table.

She had placed a white tablecloth over the dark brown wooden dinner table earlier, so she quickly went to work, setting the ten plates around the table along with the knives and forks.

Just as she was helping Jonathan bring the food out to the dinner table, there was a knock at the door. The two of them could hear their friends outside the door. Mia had told them to come before Lucas so that they could all be there to surprise him.

He had no idea that this party was happening, and Mia wanted it to be perfect.

"Come in!" she called from the dining room as she and Jonathan grabbed ten wine glasses to put on the table.

Their 6 friends – Julia, Michael, Kevin, Laura, Vivian, and Susanna – came through the door and greeted Mia and Jonathan with hugs.

"What time is he going to be here?" asked Michael as he took everyone's jackets and hung them in the hallway closet.

"He texted me a few minutes ago saying he had just picked up Thea, so they should both be here in about 5 minutes." Said Mia, practically bouncing in her excitement.

"Alright, everybody get to your spots at the table and then I will answer the door and pretend everything is normal, and then we will walk into the dining room, and all of you yell surprise." Instructed Mia.

Everyone nodded and moved to sit at the table. The excitement from everyone in the room was almost palpable. No one was speaking just in case Lucas would be able to hear them from outside.

It was not long before there was a knock on the door, and Mia could not help the giant smile that spread across her face as she went to answer the door.

She opened the door and saw her brother and Thea. Before she had time to do anything, Lucas had her in a hug.

"I missed you so much, sis." He whispered, holding her tightly.

She hugged him back just as tightly and replied, "I missed you too. I am so glad you are home."

Once they stopped hugging Mia pulled Thea into a hug as well and ushered them both inside.

Lucas saw the balloons Mia had set up and smiled, putting his arm around her shoulders as he said, "You did not have to do that."

"I know." She answered with a small smile and said, "Come on. I made dinner."

"You cooked too?" asked Lucas with a chuckle, following her into the dining room.

"Surprise!" shouted everyone.

Lucas' eyes widened in shock, but he soon had a giant smile on his face.

"You guys really did not have to go to all this trouble." He said, still smiling.

Susanna shrugged, "We just showed up. Jonathan and Mia are the ones who did all the real work."

Everyone nodded in agreement and Lucas hugged Jonathan in thanks before turning back to his sister.

"Welcome home." She said quietly, a small smile on her face.

He hugged her again and said, "You really made my favorite meal too?"

She nodded, "It is a party for you. Of course, I made your favorite."

Once everyone had settled in at the table and food had been served, everyone had a million questions for Lucas and the time he spent in Australia.

"Did you get to see any kangaroos?" asked Kevin.

Lucas nodded, "Yeah, we went on a safari the second week I was there, and we got to see all kinds of animals – kangaroos, lions, elephants, zebras – it was one of the coolest experiences of my life."

"Did you like your classes?" asked Vivian. She was the quiet bookworm out of the group, so it surprised no one that this was her question.

"Yeah, most of them. There was one class during both semesters that I did not like, but I think most of that had to do with the teacher more than the subject matter."

"What was wrong with the teacher?" asked Vivian with a raised eyebrow.

"He was just so boring. It felt like his classes would never end. Besides, it is hard to want to focus on chemistry when you are surrounded by the literal Australian wilderness." He said, looking around the table at his friends.

"I do not know how you managed to camp out there for the summer course." Shuddered Susanna. Out of everyone she was the most girlish of them all, and could not imagine ever having to spend more than a weekend camping – forget an entire summer.

Everyone around the table laughed, and Lucas said, "Well, not everyone hates the outdoors, Suzy."

"I do not *hate* the outdoors." Susanna defended.

"You just hate being out in it." Joked Mia.

Susanna said nothing but was trying – and failing – to keep the smile off her face. She knew her friends were right. They knew her well.

"Would you go back?" asked Michael.

Lucas shrugged, "Only if I could take all of you with me, or not have to be there a full year without seeing any of you."

"Aw, guys, I think he missed us." Teased Mia, a smile on her face that matched everyone else around the table.

"Yeah, yeah, yeah," Lucas said, shaking his head though he was still smiling.

"I propose a toast." Said Mia, lifting her half-filled wine glass. She waited for the others to do the same before she continued, "A toast to my brother, for pursuing his dreams and making it happen even though he was thousands of miles away from everyone he knew. We are all very proud of you."

"Cheers!" said everyone, clinking their glasses together before taking a drink.

"Now I think there is only one surprise left." Said Lucas, taking his sister's hand as he pulled her to stand from the table.

She raised an eyebrow at him, confused as she asked, "What are you talking about? There are not any other surprises..."

"Yes, there is, Mia." Said Lucas, turning her to face Jonathan, who was now on one knee in front of her.

"Oh my god, Jonathan, what are you doing?" gasped Mia, her hand going to her mouth.

"I have wanted to do this for a while now, but I knew this was a moment you would want to have your brother here for – and of course he wanted it that way too." Said Jonathan, taking Mia's hand in his while pulling a small, black velvet box from his pocket.

"I love you, Mia Safran, and there is no one else that I see myself spending the rest of my life with, but you. Will you do me the honor of marrying me?"

"Of course!" she exclaimed, a beautiful smile on her face, "I would love to marry you, Jonathan."

Everyone else cheered and clapped and whistled as Jonathan slid the ring onto her finger and kissed her.

Mia had not thought this day could possibly go as well as it had, but she was happy. Not only was her brother back home, but she was engaged.

What a day.

Conclusion

Thank you for making it through to the end of *French Short Stories for Beginners: Learn French with Short Stories and Phrases in a Fast and Revolutional Way, a Language Learning Book You Will Never Forget*; let's hope it was informative and able to provide you with all of the tools you need to achieve your goals whatever they may be.

The next step is to get your hands on more reading and workbook materials. This book is a great tool but is by no means the end all be all of French vocabulary and grammar help. It is also important to keep in mind that just because you have worked through this book once, does not mean there is nothing left to do. It may very well take you a few times of reading through each short story to really learn the words instead of just remembering the story.

Remember, there is always more to learn. Use the tips that were discussed in the first chapter to help you get the most from this book in the long run, as it has many useful vocabulary words, along with grammar you can work to emulate in your own writing.

You may find that selecting other books that have English translations available as well is still helpful, but there will certainly come a time when you will no longer need that extra help, and you will be able to get by with just a French to English dictionary.

Finally, if you found this book useful in any way, a review on Amazon is always appreciated!

FRENCH LANGUAGE FOR BEGINNERS

AN EASY STEP BY STEP GUIDE TO IMPROVE YOUR FRENCH, LEARNING NEW SKILLS WITH PHRASES AND LESSONS FROM A BASIC FRENCH TO FOREVER FLUENT

BY

LANGUAGE SCHOOL

Introduction

French is a soft, melodious and romantic language spoken by more than 200 million people in the world. It is the most widely learned language after English but also the ninth most widely spoken language in the world.

Speaking French and English is an asset in finding a job with the many French and French-speaking multinationals in diverse sectors of activity such as aeronautics, luxury or even the automotive industry. But it is also the gateway to a new culture. France shines in the world for its fashion industry, gastronomy, art, architecture and science. In reality, learning French also means being able to read in the original version the writings of great French authors such as Victor Hugo or Marcel Proust and famous poets like Charles Baudelaire. It means having the satisfaction of understanding and singing the songs of Édith Piaf or Serge Gainsbourg.

With some knowledge of French, it is so much more enjoyable to visit Paris and all the regions of France but also to understand the culture, mentalities and the French lifestyle known as "l'art de vivre à la française". Unlike popular myths, French is not a difficult language. It is a language that requires a certain precision but its richness allows you to express a multitude of nuances. You can quickly communicate in French after a few lessons and that is what this manual offers you. You will find many methods and tips to learn French while having fun.

What this book is about

Lot of French learners often get frustrated, slow down, or decide to quit. Many end up getting "left behind" simply because one aspect of the language seemed too tough or overwhelming. This guidebook will help you to eliminate some of the traps, roadblocks, and hindrances that get in your way to learning. Those learning tips are designed to make you improve and reach your goals. This book offers you the opportunity to explore different basic themes. From pronunciation to grammar and vocabulary. We've gone to the essentials in order to be accessible to all. You will find many examples and synthetic tables at each step of your progress which makes this guidebook unique and easy to use. You will have access to time-tested secrets to communication that will help you to overcome your frustration: vocabulary, grammar, and pronunciation reviews. But also proven learning tips that have helped thousands of people to improve. A simplified review that breaks the process of learning French into skill-based topics. With helpful study tips and lots of motivational advice, this book will help those falling behind to catch up and serve as a great refresher for people who are doing well in French too.

French pronunciation

The pronunciation of French letters is not always easy, it's true! Speaking and reading in French seems difficult when you start learning the language. Learning some information about letters and sounds is important to start with. This book offers general explanations, designed for beginners.

First of all, let's start with a simple fact; a sentence is made of words. Words consist of letters that form sounds. The words themselves are divided into syllables. Let's take the word FERME (Farm) as an example. The word FERME consists of two syllables FER and ME. Each syllable group forms a particular sound.

To determine the sonority of the French letters it is essential to know the alphabet. Both the French and English alphabets consist of 26 letters, including 6 vowels (A, E, I, O, U, U, Y) and 20 consonants (B, C, D, F, G, H, H, J, K, L, M, N, P, Q, R, S, T, V, W, X).

In a word vowels can be pronounced individually, but to pronounce a consonant, you will need a vowel.

The vowel can be placed after the consonant : fe, me, ma, ri etc.

The vowel can be placed before the consonant : er, ol, em, in, etc.

In order to determine more accurately the sound of consonants and vowels, you will find below three tables, using the phonetic alphabet. The phonetic alphabet is used to represent the oral language. The French language has 36 signs.

VOWELS SOUND	
[a]	a̲mi
[ɑ]	pa̲te
[ə]	le̲, je̲
[e]	e̲te̲
[ɛ]	éle̲ve, la̲i̲t
[ø]	je̲u̲
[œ]	je̲u̲ne
[i]	ami̲
[u]	po̲u̲
[o]	mo̲t, beau̲
[ɔ]	bo̲tte
[y]	lu̲ne

[ɑ̃]	d<u>an</u>s
[ɛ̃]	f<u>in</u>, m<u>ain</u>
[œ̃]	br<u>un</u>
[ɔ̃]	m<u>on</u>

CONSONANTS SOUND	
[p]	<u>p</u>ont
[b]	<u>b</u>on
[t]	<u>t</u>out
[d]	<u>d</u>eux
[k]	<u>c</u>ar, <u>qu</u>e
[g]	<u>g</u>are
[f]	<u>f</u>er
[v]	<u>v</u>erre
[s]	ba<u>ss</u>e, <u>s</u>ous
[z]	ba<u>s</u>e, <u>z</u>èbre

[ʃ]	<u>ch</u>ou
[ʒ]	<u>j</u>oue
[l]	<u>l</u>e
[R]	<u>r</u>ire
[m]	<u>m</u>on
[n]	<u>n</u>on
[ɲ]	o<u>ign</u>on

SEMI-VOYELLES ou SEMI-CONSONNES	
[j]	b<u>ill</u>e, œ<u>il</u>
[ɥ]	n<u>ui</u>t
[w]	<u>ou</u>i

The French language uses accents. The accent is not tonic, it is not used to support the sound of a letter but to modify its pronunciation.

196

- The acute accent: é. It is placed on the letter e to change its pronunciation. The sound heard is the sound [e], written é (examples: bébé/baby, école/school, télévision/television).
- The grave accent: è. It is placed on the letter e to change its pronunciation.

  The sound heard is the sound [ɛ], writes è (examples: crème/cream, père/father, mère/mother).
- The circumflex accent. It is placed on all vowels: â, ê, î, ô, û. It does not change the sound of the letter.
- The diaeresis is placed on the i and on the e: ï, ë. It indicates that the preceding vowel must be pronounced. It is therefore placed on the second vowel: ambiguïté/ambiguity (we separate u-i), maïs/corn (a-i), astéroïde/asteroid (o-i).
- The cedilla is placed under the letter c: ç. In front of a, o and u, the cedilla indicates that it should be pronounced "c" [s] and not [k]. So we can distinguish : car/because and ça/that, balcon/balcony and leçon/lesson.

French grammar

When you start learning French, you may be afraid to deal with French grammar, which is sometimes considered difficult because of its numerous exemptions rules. But in order to communicate properly, it is crucial to acquire a good grammatical knowledge. Indeed, it is impossible to separate grammar and communication. Let's take the example of a classic error: J'ai fini (meaning that you have finished an action) says something quite different than Je suis fini (meaning in familiar French that you are dead)! The only difference is in the use of the correct auxiliary verb "avoir" (have) instead of " être" (be). You can't communicate without a good knowledge of grammar. This book will explain some basic grammatical knowledge for beginner students in French.

First of all, it is necessary to distinguish the nature of a word and its function. In French, words are classified into different categories (verbs - nouns - pronouns - adjectives, etc.). Knowing the category of a word is knowing its "nature".

Example: <<Papa chante dans la cuisine>> (Daddy sings in the kitchen).

- *papa et cuisine (daddy and kitchen)* = are nouns.
- *chante (sing)* = is a verb.

And each word in a sentence has a very specific role. This role is called the "function".

Let's use the same the sentence: « Papa chante dans la cuisine».

- *Papa:* performs the action expressed by the verb "chante", so the function is "subject of the verb chante".

- *Dans la cuisine:* this group of words indicates where the action takes place, so its function is "circumstantial complement of the verb sings".

Knowing the nature of a word and its function allows you to apply the grammar rules, conjugation or syntax. For example, the subject will determine the concordance that should be done with the verb according its number (singular, plural) and genre (masculine or feminine).

Word's nature & definition

MOTS VARIABLES	DETERMINANTS	articles le, la, les, l', un, une, des	déterminants possessifs mon, ton, son, ma, ta, sa, mes, tes, ses, nos, vos, votre nos, notre, leur, leurs	déterminants interrogatifs quel quels quelle quelles déterminants démonstratifs

			ce cet cette ces
NOMS	Noms propres Paris France Seine Marie	Noms communs table fille chien fruit	
ADJECTIFS	jolie, moche, petit, grand, gros, aimable, tranquille		
VERBES	Verbe 1st groupe Aimer Regarder	Verbe 2nd groupe Dormir Punir	Verbe 3rd groupe Voir
PRONOMS	Pronoms personnels sujet J', je,	Pronoms personnels compléments lui, leur,	Pronoms relatifs qui, que

		tu, il, elle, on, nous, vous, ils, elles	eux, la, le, me, te...	
MOTS INVARIABLES	**ADVERBES**	<u>Lieu</u> Ici, ailleurs, là <u>Temps</u> Souvent, lui, hier	<u>Manière</u> Bien, mal, rapidement, vite <u>Quantité</u> Beaucoup, trop, moins, peu, très	<u>Négation</u> Ne... pas Ne.... rien Ne.... plus
	PREPOSITIONS	à, dans, par, pour, en, vers, avec, de, sans, sous		
	CONJONCTION DE COORDINATION	mais, ou, et, donc, or, ni, car		

VARIABLE & INVARIABLE WORDS:

 A variable word is a word that can be "changed". It's spelling can be different according the situation. In English, words mostly change in order to create plurals. An example of an invariable word would be "police", "information" or "sheep", those nouns does not change to the plural. In French, the definition of variable and invariable noun is the same. Words for the most part change, in order to construct plurals or feminine words. But some words will remain unchanged. For example, the words "Souvent" (Often) or "Beaucoup" (Many) will always keep the same spelling.

DETERMINERS: A determiner is a word introducing a noun like ''the'', ''a'', or ''an'' in english for example. There is just one determiner per noun and this determiner is always put before the noun. Determiners agree in gender and number with the nouns they support. In french you will find different types of determiners. ''Articles'' constitute the main group of determiners in French. You will find 3 subcategories of articles: definite, indefinite, and partitive.

Definite articles include : le, la,les. Those articles are called definite because they are used to introduce specific noun. In English, ''le'', ''la'' or ''les'' will be translated as 'the'. "Le'' is used to introduce a specific singular masculine noun. ''La'' is used to introduce a specific singular feminine noun. ''Les'' is used to introduce a specific plural noun.

Example : Juliette dessine la maison familiale. Juliette draws the family home.

Indefinite articles include : un, une,des. Those articles are named indefinite because they introduce nouns that are not specific. In English they are translated by 'a' or 'an'. ''Un'' is used to introduce a non specific singular masculine noun. ''Une'' to introduce a non specific singular feminine noun. ''Des'' is used to introduce a non specific plural noun. Example: Juliette dessine une maison. Juliette draws a house.

Partitive articles : du, de la, de l'. They are used to introduce "mass nouns", in other words nouns defined as a mass of indeterminate quantity. In English, you could translate it by "some". Example: Juliette boit du lait. Juliette drinks some milk.

Demonstrative determiners: ce,cet, cette, ces. They indicate something, usually something that can be seen. It can be translated in English as "this", "that", "these", "those", "those", "those" according the number (singular or plural). Example : Cette maison est belle. This house is beautiful. Ces chats sont petits. Those cats are small.

Possessive determiners: mon, ma,mes. They suggest ownership or possession. In English possessive determiners are : ''my'', ''your'', ''his'', ''her'', ''our'', ''their''. Example: Ma maison est petite. My house is small.

NOUNS: Nouns are words that refer to creatures, objects, abstractions or actions. They are identified in French grammar by their gender (female or male), number (singular or plural) and determinant.

VERBS: Verbs are words used to describe an activity, an interaction, an action or an event.

PRONOUNS: A pronoun is a small word used to replace a noun. For example, if I am talking about my friend Juliette, I can say: "Juliette est une artiste. Juliette peint de beaux tableaux" ("Juliette is an artist. Juliette paints beautiful artwork.").. But I could use a pronoun instead to repeat Juliette's name twice. The pronoun to choose is "she". I could say ''Juliette est une artiste. Elle peint de beaux tableaux'' ("Juliette is an artist. She paints beautiful artwork.".

ADVERBS: is an invariable word used to modify a verb, an adjective, or a noun. Adverbs provide information about the words they change, such as when, where, how much, how, etc. Nearly every French word ending in -ment is an adverb, the English equivalent would be the words ending in-ly. Like : Definitely - Définitivement. .

PREPOSITIONS: Prepositions are small words generally used with a noun or pronoun. They specify the relationships between words. Example: Juliette est allée chez Marie. Juliette went to Marie's house. Sadly, prepositions often cannot be translated in a literal way. The only solution is to look them up in a dictionary, and keep in mind the most important one. In order to help you, we created the table below. It should help you to identify more clearly the french prepositions.

à	at	for times of day	à 8 heures
	in	for spring (the season)	au printemps
		for ages or eras	au XXème siècle
	to	with *from ... to ...*	de 8 heures à 9 heures
après	after	after a certain event or time	après 8 heures
			après le cours
avant	before	before a certain event or time	avant 8 heures
			avant le cours
dans	in	in... (how long until something happens)	dans une heure
de	from	with *from ... to ...*	de 8 heures à 9 heures
			du lundi au jeudi

depuis	since, for	starting at a certain point and continuing until now	depuis 1980
			depuis 2 ans
dès	since	starting at a certain point and continuing until now	dès 8 heures
			dès lundi
en	in	months	en février
		all seasons except for spring	en été, en automne, en hiver
	in	years	en 2008
jusque	until	until a certain point	jusqu'en février
pendant	during, for...	to indicate how long something lasts	pendant les vacances b
			pendant trois jours

COORDINATING CONJUNCTIONS : In French you will find 7 coordinating conjunctions: "mais", "ou", "et", "donc", "or", "ni", "car" ("but", "or", "and", "therefore", "so", "therefore", "because"). These are invariant words that are used to join words together. The examples below should help you to better understand their meaning and use.

Conjunctions	English translations	Examples
mais	but	J'aime les fruits mais pas la viande. *I like fruits but not meat.*
ou	or	Tu iras en France ou en Allemagne pour travailler. *You will go in France or in Germany to work.*
et	and	Jeanne et Julien sont mignons. *Jeanne and Julien are cute.*
donc	so, therefore	Elle a cinq ans, donc c'est encore un enfant. She is five years old, so she's still a child.
or	now, yet	Je n'aime pas la chaleur, or je vis dans le sud de la France.

		I don't like the heat, yet I live in the south of France.
ni	neither... nor	Il n'aime ni la viande, ni les légumes. *He doesn't like meat nor vegetables.*
car	because	Il vient au cinéma car il aime regarder des films. *He comes to the cinema because he likes watching movies.*

Now we defined the basic vocabulary, we will briefly and synthetically approach some French grammar rules that will help you to improve your language skills. However, most of the grammar rules listed below will be studied in more detail, later in this book.

Nouns: the plural specificities

How to turn a singular french noun into a plural noun? In general you will create a plural noun by adding at the end of a noun the letter "s". Sometimes it will be "aux". You will find below some example.

As we said previously, adding a "s" at the end of a singular noun turns it into a plural noun.

- For example : The word **Pomme** (*apple*) becomes **Pommes** (*apples*). The word **Maison** (*house*) becomes **Maisons** (*houses*).

Some nouns might take a "x" at the end in order to become a plural noun. In general you can identify those nouns easily because they end up with "au" or "al" in the singular. In order to become plural they have to drop the "al" or the "au" to use "aux".

- For example : The word **Cheval** (house) becomes **Chevaux** (horses). The word **Journal** (newspaper) becomes **Journaux** (newspapers). Bateau (boat) becomes Bateaux (boats).

Nouns ending in "**ou**" will finish in "**s**" in the plural, but some take "**x**".

- For example: **Hibou** (*owl*) becomes **Hiboux** (*owls*), and **Genou** (*knee*) becomes **Genoux** (*knees*), **Joujou** (toy) becomes **Joujoux** (toys).

Nouns ending in "**s**", "z" or "**x**" in the singular remain the same in the plural. But remember, you have to change the accompanying article.

- For example: **un Anglais** (*an Englishman*) remains **des Anglais** (*Englishmen*), and **un corps** (*a body*) remains **des corps** (*bodys*).

Nouns: The gender specificities.

There is a particularity in French, which you will not find in English. We are talking about the grammatical gender of words. This may seem challenging for any English-speaking person who wants to learn French. Indeed, in English names do not have a gender, when we talk about a house, a fruit, a car no gender applies. However in French the words have a gender and you will learn that if house (maison) and car (voiture) are feminine words, fruit (fruit) is a masculine word. Indeed, the ending of an adjective changes according to the gender of the word to which it refers. For example, any adjective associated to a feminine noun must also be written in its feminine form. And it's the same thing for the article placed before that noun, it also have to be spelled in its feminine form.

For example: *Une fille forte* (A strong girl). *Un* garçon *fort* (A strong boy)

When you start learning French, it is helpful to remember the gender of the words you're studying. Indeed, it will be very useful to know the gender of the words later on in order for example to pick the right pronoun or determinant etc. But also in order to write correctly your adjectives according the noun they refer to. Maison (house) is a female word. We will say : La maison est belle (the house is beautiful). Belle is the feminine form of the word beautiful. The word coussin (cushion) is masculine, we will say: Le coussin est beau (the cushion is beautiful). Beau is the masculine form of the word beautiful. There are many tips for learning the nouns gender in French. Below is a list of nouns, whose endings are typically associated with one or the other gender.

For example, the nouns with the following endings are in general feminine:

- words ending with a vowel, followed by a consonant (or two) then "e," like: *-ine, -ane, -ome, -alle, -elle, -esse, -ette, -euse, -ance, -ence...*
- *-tion, -son, -sion*
- *-ée, -té, -ière*
- *-ude, -ure, -ade*

The nouns with the following endings are in general masculine :

- *-ste* and *-tre*
- *-u, -oir, -ou*
- *-me, -ment, -isme*
- *-age* and *-ege*
- *-eur* and *-eau*
- *-ble* and *-cle*
- Consonants: *-b, -c, -d, -f, -k, -l, -m, -n, -p, -r, -s, -t, -x*

Keep in mind that there are always some exceptions that you should learn specifically, but this template is a useful guideline. Another effective way to learn the gender of a new word would be to learn sentences suggesting the gender, or by connecting words of the same gender and learning them together, like : l'homme promène son chien dans le jardin (The man walks his dog in his yard) ou La femme regarde la télévision dans la maison (The woman watches television in the house).

In a similar vein, when you are learning thematic vocabulary lists, divide the words into a list of male words and a list of female words. For example, when you learn about nature, you can have forest (forêt) and mountain (montagne) which are feminine words in one list and tree (arbre) and sky (ciel) which are masculine words in another. Try to picture those words and create a mental image of these things that you could recall later.

Basic verb knowledge, HAVE and BE.

When you learn French, it is recommended to learn in priority two verbs. The verb AVOIR (to have) and the verb ÊTRE (to be) because they are the most commonly used verbs in the French language. Indeed, they are the foundation of everyday communication, and will allow you to express a large amount of information.

Let's take a look at them:

TO HAVE - present tense	AVOIR — temps present
I have	J'ai
You have	Tu as
He/she has	Il/elle/on a
We have	Nous avons
You have	Vous avez
They have	Ils/elles ont

TO BE - present tense	ÊTRE — temps present
I am a	Je suis
You are	Tu es
He/she is	Il/elle/on est
We are	Nous sommes
You are	Vous êtes
They are	Ils/elles sont

Mastering both verbs in the present tense, in the past but also in the future is a very good idea, and will help you to facilitate your communication.

Negative sentences

This is a part of French grammar that is very useful to practice and apply. It's not difficult to form negative sentences in French, but it will allow you to instantly multiply what you can express in your new language by two.

So now you can say: "Je veux des fleurs" (I want flowers). But if, for some mysterious reason, you want to say the opposite, all you have to do is use the negotiation rules and say "Je ne veux pas des fleurs" (I don't want flowers). All you should do is adding' 'ne" before the verb and "pas" after the verb. In short, you will just have to use the structure **ne + [verb] + not.**

Another example: "Je parle Chinois" (I speak Chinese) becomes "Je ne parle pas Chinois" (I don't speak Chinese). Remember if your verb starts with a vowel, you will have to use *n'* instead of *ne*. For example : "J'aime les gâteaux" (I like cakes) becomes "Je n'aime pas les gâteaux" (I don't like cakes).

Pas (don't) is the most common word used to express the negation but you can change *pas* to other words allowing you to describe different nuances of negation. For example, you could use the word *plus* (don't....anymore) or *jamais* (never). It is not uncommon to hear sentences containing this type of negation, such as: *Il ne ment jamais.* He never lies. Or: *Tu ne manges plus de viande.* You don't like meat anymore.

French grammar is known to be challenging, but you only have to start studying to understand that it is not as complicated as you thought. Learning grammar requires a little discipline and organization, but once you start learning, everything is setting up quickly and makes sense. Even if this is not the funniest part, it is a solid foundation that will allow you to become more efficient and better in French. If you learn these basics, speaking French will become a piece of cake.

Numbers, days, months, seasons

It is essential to know numbers, days, months and seasons in order to be able to express an infinite range of ideas and information. Indeed, knowing these basics will not only allow you to say a little more about yourself, but it will also help you to communicate better with your Francophone environment. Being able to express an idea of temporality or quantity is essential in everyday life. Whether it is to do shopping, asking for a price, telling the time, the date, the address, the age, the temperature, etc. You will therefore find below the basis of this knowledge in the form of a concise and quick table. Of course we will teach you how to apply this new vocabulary in a simple and effective way.

Numbers in French

NUMBERS	NOMBRES
0 : zero 1: one 2: two	0 : zéro 1 : un 2 : deux

3: three	3 : trois
4: four	4 : quatre
5: five	5 : cinq
6: six	6 : six
7: seven	7 : sept
8: eight	8 : huit
9: new	9 : neuf
10: ten	10 : dix
11: eleven	11 : onze
12: twelve	12 : douze
13: thirteen	13 : treize
14: fourteen	14 : quatorze
15: fifteen	15 : quinze
16: sixteen	16 : seize
17: seventeen	17 : dix-sept
18: eighteen	18 : dix-huit
19: nineteen	19 : dix-neuf
20: twenty	20 : vingt
21: twenty-one	21 : vingt et un
22: twenty-two	22 : vingt-deux
23: twenty-three	23 : vingt-trois
24: twenty-four	24 : vingt-quatre
25: twenty-five	25 : vingt-cinq
26: twenty-six	26 : vingt-six
27: twenty-seven	27 : vingt-sept

28: twenty-eight	28 : vingt-huit
29: twenty-nine	29 : vingt-neuf
30: thirty	30 : trente
40: forty	40 : quarante
50: fifty	50 : cinquante
60: sixty	60 : soixante
70: seventy	70 : soixante-dix
80: eighty	80 : quatre-vingts
90: Ninety	90 : quatre-vingt-dix
100: one hundred	100 : cent
1,000: one thousand	1 000 : mille
1,000,000: one million	1 000 000 : un million

Days, Months and Seasons

DAYS OF THE WEEK	JOURS DE LA SEMAINE
Monday	Lundi
Tuesday	Mardi
Wednesday	Mercredi
Thursday	Jeudi
Friday	Vendredi
Saturday	Samedi

| Sunday | Dimanche |

MONTHS	MOIS
January	Janvier
February	Février
March	Mars
April	Avril
May	Mai
June	Juin
July	Juillet
August	Août
September	Septembre
October	Octobre
November	Novembre
December	Décembre

SEASONS	SAISONS
Springtime	Printemps
Autumn	Automne
Summer	Été
Winter	Hiver

Now that you have learned the vocabulary listed above, let's learn some simple rules to help you to incorporate this vocabulary into sentences.

Rule 1. We use the verb to be (ETRE) to ask for the date.
Examples :

- *Quel jour sommes-nous ?* Literally it could be translated by: Which day are we today? In English the right translation is: What day is it today?

- *Nous sommes le 10 septembre 2019.* Literally it could be translated by: We are the 10 September 2019? In English the right translation is: It is September 10, 2019.

Rule 2. The day is written with the article defined LE (the) + le chiffre du jour (day's number) + mois (month) + année (year/optional).
Examples :

- Je suis né le 5 janvier 1990. I was born on January 5, 1990.

- Nous partons le 10 juin en France. We leave for France on June 10.

- Ils reviennent le 20 octobre de Paris. They come back from Paris on October 20.

Rule 3. To give a date (month and year) without specifying the day, use the preposition *en* (in).
Examples :

- Je suis né en Mars. I was born in March.

- Je suis né <u>en</u> 1991. I was born in 1991.

- Je suis née <u>en</u> Mars 1991. I was born in March 1991.

Rule 4. To talk about a day, we don't use a preposition.

Examples :

- Je suis arrivé lundi matin. I arrived Monday morning.

- Nous allons au spa mardi prochain. We're going to the spa next Tuesday.

Nouns and articles (common nouns, articles and rules)

The French Article

In the French language, articles are sometimes confusing for students because they must be in agreement with the nouns they accompany. Generally, in front of a noun, there is always an article or an other type of determinant such as a possessive determiner (*mon* (my), *your* (ton)...) or a demonstrative determiner (*ce, cette* (this)...).

In French there is three types of articles:

- First, the definite articles.
- Second, the indefinite articles.
- Third, the partitive articles.

French Articles			
	Definite	*Indefinite*	*Partitive*
Masculine	le	un	du
Feminine	la	une	de la
In front of a vowel	l'	un/une	de l'
Plural	les	des	des

French definite article

The definite article in French would be translated by "the" in English. You can spell ''the'' in French in four differents way.

1. le   (in front of a masculine singular noun)
2. la   (in front of a feminine singular noun)
3. l'   (in front of a masculine or feminine noun starting with a vowel or a silent h)

4. les (in front of a masculine or feminine plural noun)

In short, if you wonder which one to use, you should identify the noun's gender, number, and its first letter. For a plural noun, you have to use ''les''. For a singular noun beginning with a vowel or a silent *h*, you have to use ''l'''. For a singular masculine noun you have to use ''le''. For a singular feminine noun you have to use ''la''.

The definite article is used if front of a specific noun, for something definite, particular. For instance: *Je vais a l'ecole* (I'm going to school). *C'est le sac que j'ai acheté* (This is the bag I bought).

The defined article is also used in the French language to express the overall meaning of a noun. This can be misleading, as the defined articles are not used this way in the English language. For example: *J'aime le fromage* / I like cheese.

French Indefinite Articles

The indefinite articles in English could be translated by "a," "an," or "one" at the singular, while the plural could be translated by "some." You can find three types of indefinite article in french.

1. un   (in front of a singular masculine noun)
2. une (in front of a singular feminine noun)
3. des (in front of a masculine or feminine plural noun)

The plural indefinite article never change, at the opposite of the the singular indefinite article that change if the noun they precede is masculine or feminine.

The indefinite article is in general used to refers to a non specific person or object. For example: *J'ai vu un chien* (I saw a dog). Sometimes the indefinite article can be used to refer to the number "one". For example: *J'ai un chat et trois chiens* (I have one cat and three dogs). The plural indefinite article are in general not translated in English. For example: *J'ai acheté des livres* (I bought books).

In English when you talk about a person's profession, you will use the indefinite article. But not in French. For example: *Je suis docteur* (I am a doctor).

In a sentence including a negation, the indefinite article "un" or "une" will become "de". For example: *J'ai une voiture / Je n'ai pas de voiture (*I have a car / I don't have any car).

French Partitive Articles

The partitive articles could be translated in English by "some" or "any". You can find four types of partitive article:

1. du   (in front of a masculine singular noun)
2. de la (in front of a feminine singular noun)
3. de l' (in front of a masculine or feminine noun starting with a vowel or a silent h)
4. des   (for a plural noun, masculine or feminine)

As you understood, the choice of the right article will depend on the number, gender and first letter of the noun it precedes: So if the noun is plural, you will choose des. If it's a singular noun beginning with a vowel or a silent *h*, use "de l'". If it's a singular masculine noun you will have to choose "du", same for the nouns starting with a consonant and for a feminine singular noun you will choose "de la".

The partial article is used to express an unknown amount of something, usually drink or food. For example: *Avez-vous de l'eau?* (Do you have some water?). *Nous mangeons de la tarte* (We eat some pie). *Je mange du pain* (I eat some bread).

After any adverbs expressing quantity, you should use "de". For example: *Il y a beaucoup de café* (There is a lot of coffee). *Tu as moins de temps pour finir ton devoir* (You have less time to complete your homework).

The French Nouns

All nouns in the French language have a gender which can be masculine or feminine. In many cases, you will have to memorize the gender of the nouns. But there are a few word endings that give you a hind regarding the gender. For example, nouns ending in -age and -ment are mostly masculine. Names ending in -ure, -tion, -sion, -ance, -ence, -té and -ette are typically feminine.

Adjectives and articles shall agree in number and gender with the nouns they change.

Masculine	Feminine	Before Vowel	Plural
le sac the bag	**la** bague the ring	**l'**aigle the eagle	**les** robes the dresses

Masculine	Feminine	Plural
un sac a bag	**une** bague a ring	**des** robes some dresses

Masculine	Masculine, Before Vowel	Feminine	Plural
ce sac *this/that bag*	**cette** bague *this/that ring*	**cet** aigle *this/that eagle*	**ces** robes *these/those dresses*

Plural Nouns

	Singular	Plural
To create plural, you just have to add a -s at the end of a noun (which is "silent"). It's a general rule, but there are also some exceptions:	*Singular*	*Plural*
If the noun already finishes with -s, nothing has to be added	*notice (es)*	**l'avis**	**les avis**
If the noun finishes with -eau you should change it for -x at the end in order	*raft(s)*	**le radeau**	**les radeaux**

to turn a singular noun into a plural noun.			
If a *masculine* noun finishes in -al or -ail, you should change it for -aux in order to construct a plural noun.	*pet(s)*	**l'ani mal**	**les anim aux**
For nouns ending in -ou, you should add a -x or a -s at the end.	*Owl(s)*	**le hibo u**	**les hibo ux**

There are particular exceptions, like: carnaval, festival, bal, bleu, pneu, landau, détail, chandail (carnival, festival, ball, blue, tire, pram, detail, sweater) all add -s. You have only seven nouns ending with -ou that add -x and not -s in order to construct the plural : bijou, chou, caillou, genou, joujou, pou, hibou (jewelry, cabbage, pebble, knee, toy, louse, owl). On the top of that, you should know there are, of course, few irregular cases : œil (eye) becomes yeux (eyes); ciel (sky) becomes cieux (skies).

Useful French Nouns Listing:

You will find below a list of the most common nouns, organized by category in order to develop your vocabulary in the best and most efficient way.

CATEGORY : FRUIT		CATEGORY : NATURE		CATEGORY : ANIMAL	
pomme	apple	herbe	grass	renard	fox
poire	pear	forêt	forest	loup	wolf
pêche	peach	plaine	lowland	chien	dog
fraise	strawber	montag	mountai	chat	cat
citron	ry	ne	n	girafe	giraffe
banane	lemon	lac	lake	éléphant	Elephan
melon	banana	fleur	flower	lion	t
pasteque	melon	légume	vegetabl	tigre	lion
e	waterme	feuille	e	singe	tiger
cerise	lon	sapin	leaf	poisson	monkey
abricot	cherry	olivier	fir tree	dauphin	fish
ananas	apricot	pivoine	olive	requin	dolphin
mague	pineappl	marguer	tree	koala	shark
raisin	e	ite	peony	ours	koala
framboi	mango	champ	daisy	cerf	bears
se	grape	campag	field	lapin	deer
kiwi	raspberr	ne	countrys	souris	rabbit
	y	bois	ide		mouse
	kiwi		wood		

CATEGORY : FAMILY		CATEGORY : WORK		CATEGORY : TIME	
mère	mother	herbe	grass	avant	right now
maman	mommy	forêt	forest	après	before
père	father	plaine	lowland	toujours	after
papa	daddy	montagne	mountain	tout le temps	always
copine	girl	lac	lake	il était	all the time
fils	son	fleur	flower	une fois	once upon a time
tante	aunt	légume	vegetable	lendemain	tomorrow
oncle	uncle	feuille	leaf	la semaine prochaine	next week
grand-mère	grandmother	sapin	fir tree	saison	season
grand-père	grandfather	olivier	olive tree	automne	fall
cousin	cousin	pivoine	peony	printemps	springtime
neveu	nephew	marguerite	daisy	été	summer
nièce	niece	champ	field	hiver	wintertime
sœur	sister	campagne	countryside	siècle	century
frère	brother	bois	wood	millénai	millennium
enfant	child	feu	fire		year
bébé	baby	vent	wind		
		terre	earth		

				re année	

Adjectives (common adjectives and rules)

French Adjectives and Rules

The adjective is a word bringing a precision about a noun or a pronoun. Just like in English, an adjective helps to specify a noun or a pronoun, by assigning a quality or a defect. For example: Cet homme est *gentil* mais il est *ennuyeux* (This man is *kind* but he is *boring*). Or by allowing to precise an information. For example : Le *premier* joueur a gagne (The *first* player has won).

As we said, the adjective always refers to a noun or pronoun with which it agrees in gender (masculine or feminine) and number (singular or plural).

For example in the sentence: Il est intelligent/He is smart, the adjective ***intelligent*** (smart) is masculine singular because it agrees with the subject pronoun *il* (he) which is masculine, singular. In the sentence: Elles sont intelligentes / They are smart, the adjective ***intelligentes*** is plural feminine because it agrees with the subject pronoun *elles* (they) which is feminine, plural.

In other words, the adjective should always reflect the gender and the number of nouns it modifies.

Gender:

As you know nouns in French have a gender. If you want to talk about a male noun, like le bureau (the desk), you will need to use an adjective written in masculine, singular to associate with your masculine singular noun. So if you want to describe the color of your desk, which is grey for example, you will talk about *un bureau **gris*** (a grey desk). But if you want to talk about your grey car you will have to spell grey in feminine singular, because the noun car in french is feminine, singular. So you will say: *Une voiture **grise**.* Please note that the feminine version of gris has an *e* at the end. It's the traditional way to create the feminine termination.

Number:

In French a noun may be singular or plural, whatever the gender, the adjective has to correspond to this. If you want to talk about many grey cars you will say : *Des voitures **grises**.*

Please note that the adjective took an *s* at the end. As you might know it's the traditional way to build the plural.

You will find below some general rules about how to turn a masculine singular adjective into a feminine singular adjective:

- The most traditional way to turn a masculine adjective into a feminine adjective is to add an −**e** at the end of its masculine singular form.
- For the masculine singular adjectives already ending in −**e**, they remain as it is. Do not add an extra -e. For instance, **drole** (*funny*), **mince** (*thin*), and **calme** (*calm*) remain the same in masculine singular and in feminine singular.
- For most part of the adjectives ending with a vowel and a consonant, you have to double that consonant before adding −**e** in order to create the feminine termination. For instance: **ancien** (*old*) becomes **ancienne**, **actuel** (*current*) becomes **actuelle.**
- For the adjectives ending in −**eux**, or -**eur** you should replace this termination with−**euse** in order to get a feminine termination. For example: **heureux** (*happy*) becomes **heureuse**, **menteur** (*liar*) becomes **menteuse**, **ambitieux** (*ambitious*) becomes **ambitieuse** and so on.
- For the adjectives ending in −**teur**, you should replace this termination with −**trice** to create the feminine. For

instance: **Amateur** (hobbyist) becomes **amatrice**, **protecteur** (*protector*) becomes **protectrice**, etc.

- For the adjectives ending in −**er**, you should replace this termination with −**ère** to create the feminine, like **leger** (*light*) to **legère**, **fier** (*proud*) to **fière**, and **amer** (*bitter*) to **amère.**

- For the adjectives ending in −**et**, you should replace this termination with −**ète** to build the feminine. For example, **concret** (*concrete*) becomes **concrète**, **desuet** (*old-fashioned*) becomes **desuète**, and **complet** (*complete*) becomes **complète**.

- For the adjectives ending in −**f,** you should replace this termination with −**ve** to form the feminine, for instance **veuf** (*widower*) becomes **veuve**, and **tardif** (*late*) becomes **tardive**.

- For the adjectives describing nationality and ending in −**ain**, like **Dominicain** (*Dominican*) or **Americain** (*American*) add an -e without doubling the −**n.**

You will find below some general rules about how to turn a singular adjective into a plural adjective:

- The traditional way of creating the plural of an adjective is by adding an −**s** to the masculine or the feminine form. For instance, the masculine singular adjective **noir** (*black*) becomes **noirs** in plural, and the feminine singular **noire** (*black*) becomes **noires** in plural.

- For the adjective already ending with –**s** or –**x** at the masculine singular, In general you don't have to add another–**s** to form plural. The adjective remains the same for the masculine plural. For example: **Nerveux** (*nervous*) is spelled the same way for the singular or for the plural. Same for **gros** (*big*) or **gris** (*grey*).
- For the masculine singular adjectives ending in –**al**, replace it with –**aux** to form the plural. For instance, **égal** (*equal*) becomes **égaux** (*equals*) in plural.
- For the masculine singular adjectives ending in –**eau**, add a –**x** at the end to create plural. For instance, **nouveau** (*new*) becomes **nouveaux** *(news)* in the plural, and **beau** (*beautiful*) becomes **beaux** *(beautifuls)*.
- The masculine singular adjective **tout** (*all*) turns into **tous** in the masculine plural.

Common French Adjectives Listing

Here is a list of popular adjectives describing the look, the personality and the feelings. The red terminations next some of the adjective below, are the feminine termination of the adjective. In other word, you will need to switch the masculine termination for the red termination to get the feminine form of the adjective. Those that do not have a specification, remain unchanged (it's the case of adjectives ending with -e) or just need a "e" at the end in order to create the feminine version of the adjective.

LOOK	ALLURE	PERSONALITY	PERSONNALITÉ	FEELINGS	SENTIMENTS
Adorable	Adorable	Aggressive	Agressif -ive	In love	Amoureux -euse
Attractive	Attrayant	Ambitious	Ambitieux -euse	Anxious	Anxieux -euse
Beautiful	Beau	Miser	Avare	Drunk	Bourru
Confident	Belle	Brave	Brave	Calm	Calme
Strong	Confiant	Temperamental	Caracteriel -elle	Happy	Content
Soft	Costaud	Warm	Chaleureux-euse	Naughty	Coquin
Elegant	Doux -ouce	Cruel	Cruel	Guilty	Coupable
Large	Elegant	Dangerous	Dangereux -euse	Depressed	Déprimé
Big	Grand	Unpleasant	Désagréable	Painful	Douloureux -euse
Hideous	Gros	Determined	Déterminé	Scared	Effrayé
Concerned	Hideux -euse	Gifted	Doué	Angry	En colère
Magnificent	Inquiet	Selfish	Egoiste	Boring	Ennuyeux -euse
Lean	Magnifique	Deceitful	Fourbe		Envieux -euse
Clumsy	Maigre				Épuisé
Wonderful	Maladroit				Furax

Thin	Merveilleux -euse	Generous	Généreux -euse	Envious	Faible
Perfect	Mince	Hypocrite	Hypocrite	Exhausted	Fidèle
Clean	Parfait	Idiot	Idiot	Mad	Fier
Small	Propre	Clever	Intelligent	Weak	Heureux -euse
Dirty	Petit	Jealous	Jaloux -louse	Faithful	Honteux -euse
Wild	Sale	Foolish	Loufoque	Proud	Malicieux -euse
Attractive	Sauvage	Mysterious	Mystérieux -euse	Happy	Malade
Dark	Séduisant	Mean	Méchant	Ashamed	Mauvais
Smiling	Sombre	Punctual	Ponctuel	Malicious	Prétentieux -euse
Shy	Souriant	Wise	Sage	Sick	Prudent
Lively	Timide	Sincere	Sincère	Bad	Triste
	Vif -Vive	Spiritual	Spirituel	Pretentious	Troublé
		Naughty	Vilain	Prudent	Tranquille
		Old	Vieux Vieille	Sad	
				Troubled	
				Quiet	

The following list is showing popular adjectives describing shape, size, time and quantity. The red terminations next some of the adjective below, are the feminine termination of the adjective. In other word, you will need to switch the masculine termination for the red termination to get the feminine form of the adjective. Those that do not have a specification, remain unchanged (it's the case of adjectives ending with -e) or just need a "e" at the end in order to create the feminine version of the adjective.

SHAPE	FORME	SIZE	TAILLE
Altered	Altéré	Colossal	Colossal
Square	Carré	Significant	Considérable
Circular	Circulaire	Huge	Enorme
Hollow	Creux -euse	Exiguous	Exigu
Decomposed	Décomposé	Thin	Fin
Deformed	Déformé	Gigantic	Gigantesque
Right	Droit	Large	Grand
Narrow	Étroit	Huge	Immense
Geometrics	Géométrique	Important	Important
Wide	Large	Imposing	Imposant
Long	Long -gue	Tiny	Infime
Lean	Maigre	Wide	Large
Flat	Plat	Slim	Menu
Primitive	Primitif -ive	Microscopic	Minuscule
Stiff	Raide	Monumental	Monumental
Rectangular	Rectangulair	Small	Petit
Round	e	Spacious	Spacieux
Simple	Rond	Great	Super
Twisted	Simple	Extensive	Vaste
Triangular	Tordu		
	Triangulaire		

TIME	TEMPS	QUANTITY	QUANTITÉ
Current	Actuel -elle	abundant	abondant
Former	Ancien -enne	compact	compact
Annual	Annuel -elle	significant	considérable
Ancient	Antique	dense	dense
Advanced	Avancé	huge	énorme
Weekly	Hebdomadai	frequent	fréquent
Young	re	unlimited	illimité
Daily	Jeune	invaluable	incalculable
Slow	Journalier	countless	innombrable
Monthly	Lent	lightweight	léger -ère
Modern	Mensuel	heavy	lourd
Brand-new	Moderne	diverse	multiple
New	Neuf -euve	numerous	nombreux
Rushed	Nouveau -elle	filled out	rempli
Prompt	Précipité	significant	substantiel
Fast	Prompt	repeted	répété
Late	Rapide	empty	vide
Old-	Tardif -ive	voluminous	volumineux -
fashioned	Vétuste		euse

Here is a list of popular adjectives describing the
sound, the taste, the touch and the color. The red

terminations next some of the adjective below, are the feminine termination of the adjective. In other word, you will need to switch the masculine termination for the red termination to get the feminine form of the adjective. Those that do not have a specification, remain unchanged (it's the case of adjectives ending with -e) or just need a "e" at the end in order to create the feminine version of the adjective.

SOUND	SON	TASTE	GOUT
acute	aigu	acrid	âcre
deafening	assourdissant	enjoyable	agréable
bawling	beuglant	sour	aigre
noisy	bruyant	bitter	amer amère
light	clair	delicious	délectable
soft	doux douce	smooth	douceâtre
squeaky	grinçant	spicy	épicé
matt	mat	exquisite	exquis
melancholic	mélancolique	bland	fade
piercing	perçant	fresh	frais fraîche
pointed	pointu	icy	glacé
whispering	chuchoté	tasty	goûteux -euse
resounding	retentissant	tasteless	insipide
cooing	roucoulant	juicy	juteux -euse
silent	silencieux -	salty	salé
deaf	euse	delightful	succulent
shrill	sourd	sweet	sucré
thunderous	strident		
	tonnant		

TOUCH	TOUCHER	COLOR	COULEUR
rugged	accidenté	silver	argenté
sticky	collant	white	blanc blanche
soft	doux douce	blue	bleu
harsh	dur	beige	beige
scattered	éparpillé	blond	blond
firm	ferme	brown	brun
slippery	glissant	grey	grise
inconsistent	inégal	yellow	jaune
mellow	moelleux	brown	marron
weak slack	mou molle	black	noir
wet	mouillé	orange	orange
hot	piquant	pink	rose
pointed	pointu	redhead	roux rousse
sandy	sableux euse	red	rouge
dry	sec sèche	turquoise	turquoise
flexible	souple	green	vert
tender	tendre	purple	violet
		black	noir

Position Of French Adjectives

Most of the French adjectives describing the features of a noun are positioned after that noun. However, some adjectives may be placed before the noun they describe, and some may go either before or after, depending on their significance. French adjectives placed after the nouns they describe: In general, and in contrast to English, French adjectives are located after the noun they describe. Below are some adjectives illustrating this difference:

-Une robe rose (a pink dress).

Un sourire éclatant (a bright smile).

-Des gâteaux sucrés (some sweet cakes).

In the examples above, the adjectives are rose (pink), éclatant (bright), and sucrés (sweet).

French adjectives placed before the nouns they describe: Adjectives relating to particular qualities shall precede the noun they describe. Those qualities can be summarized by the acronym BAGS:

- B stands for beauty: **joli** (*pretty*), **beau** (*beautiful*)
- A stands for age: **vieux** (*old*), **jeune** (*young*), **nouveau** (*new*)
- G stands for goodness: **meilleur** (*better*), **bon** (*good*), **gentil** (*kind*), **mauvais** (*bad*)
- S stands for size: **haut** (*high*), **petit** (*small*), **gros** (*fat*)

Only few adjectives referring to the qualities included in the BAGS acronym are placed after the noun they describe. For the adjectives referring to the beauty, the exceptions are **affreux** (*atrocious*) and **laid** or **moche** (*ugly*); for the adjectives referring to the age, the exception is **âgé** (*old*); and for the adjectives referring to the goodness, the exception is **méchant** (*mean*). For instance: **une peinture moche** (*an ugly paint*), **des dames âgées** (*old ladies*), **un enfant méchant** (*a mean child*).

Regarding ordinal adjectives — which are adjectives describing the order in which things come — they are placed before nouns. For examples: **Le premier enfant de Claude est Marine.** (*Claude's first child is Marine*). **Nous habitons au second étage.** (*We live on the second floor*). **C'est la dernière fois que tu arrives en retard.** (*This is the last time you'll be late*).

The adjective **tout** (*all* or *every* in English) precedes the noun and also the article. Please note, we spell **tout** for the masculine singular, **toute** for the feminine singular, and **tous** for the plural. For instance :

-**Il pleut tout le temps,** (*It rains all the time*).

-**Elle mange toute la journée,** (*She eats all day long*).

-**Tu chantes tous les jours,** (*You sing every day*).

-**Toutes les femmes sont belles,** (*All the women are beautiful*).

The adjectives **tel** (*such*), **autre** (*other*), **faux** (*false*) and **même** (*same*), should also be placed before the nouns.

Examples:

-**Je voudrais une autre part de gâteau,** (*I'd like another piece of cake*).　　　　　　　　　 -**Une fausse réponse,** (*A false answer*).

Adjectives with changing meaning according to their position, before or after the noun.

Some adjectives can be placed before or after the noun, according what they mean. Typically if you need to express a literal meaning, you need to place the adjective after the noun but if you need to express a more figurative meaning, you should place it before.

Adjectives	Before the noun - English translation	After the noun - English translation

Ancien	Former	Antique, Old
Certain	Some	Sure
Cher	Dear	Expensive
Dernier	Final	Previous, Last (regarding time)
Grand	Great	Tall
Pauvre	Wretched, Miserable	Poor, Broke
Propre	My own	Clean
Seul	Only	Alone
Simple	Mere	Simple

Examples:

Le dernier jour des vacances est mardi. (*The last day of the holidays is Tuesday..*)

Mardi dernier, je suis retourné à l'école. (*Last Tuesday, I went back to school.*)

Ces pauvres enfants sont fatigués. (*These poor children are tired.*)

Ces enfants sont pauvres. (*These children are poor.*)

Son ancien mari s'est remarié. (*Her ex-husband remarried.*)

Sa bague est ancienne. (*Her ring is antique.*)

Pronouns and verbs (commons pronouns, verbs and rules)
French personal pronouns

Personal pronouns are essential to the French language, so it is very important to familiarize yourself with them. However, there are various types of pronouns. The personal pronouns are those such as "I", "you", "he", "she", "it", "we", or "they". They are used as the subject of a specific sentence. The French and English pronouns vary slightly in terms of type and use, so it is extremely important to understand the distinctions. Although even if they may appear simple at first, French personal pronouns can not always been translated directly in English, it's the reason why it's important to pay particular attention to them.

Let's take a look:

- Je - I
- Tu - You
- Il/elle/on - He/She/We
- Nous - We
- Vous - You, formal or plural
- Ils/elles - They

In France it's essential to learn the difference between tu (informal *you*) and vous (formal *you*). It's a serious matter for french people. While you spoke to your relatives, family members, or friends you will use tu (informal *you*). But when you talk to strangers, authority figures or elders you will use vous (formal *you*).

Likewise, there is also a difference between on (*we* or *one*) and nous (*we*) which deserves to be looked at. On can mean "*we*" or "*one*". Nous are only used to express "*we*". In French, we use sometimes more on than nous, it's a familiar, contemporary way to talk.

Reflexive verbs

Reflexive verbs are used to talk about what people do to "themselves". You will find many examples took from everyday life.

In the English language, someone could say *I wake-up myself*. This is considered as a reflexive verb, because it relates to something that we do to "ourselves". In French, reflexive verbs are slightly different. For example, in order to say *I wake-up myself*, French people would say: **je me réveilles**. In a literal way it would be: *I myself wake-up*. **Me** is the reflexive part, because it relates to who the action is done. If you meant: *you wake-up yourself*, you would say **tu te réveilles**. The reflexive would be **te** (yourself). It is not complicated to remember how to turn a pronoun into its reflexive form. You will find below the matching reflexive pronouns for each personal pronoun:

- Je : **me**
- Tu : **te**
- Il/elle/on : **se**
- Nous : **nous**
- Vous : **vous**
- Ils/elles : **se**

Many reflexive verbs are taught as being part of actions from everyday life or actions taking place at home, although there are many varieties of reflexive verbs. The words **brosser** (*brush*), **laver** (*wash*) or **aller se coucher** (*go to bed*) can all take the reflective form, and are in general the most commonly used. Reflexive verbs in French may seem a bit strange at first, but if you check them regularly, they will soon come to you quite easily.

French verbs, conjugations and rules

When you start to learn French conjugation, regular verbs are your best friends. Trying to memorize the terminations of regular verb in the present tense does not take much time at all. You will be able to use the most popular verbs easily and without to much effort. It's the reason why conjugation is something you should take a loot at, very early on. And for the people who wonder what conjugation is about, in short, it's how a verb is written to be in agreement with the main subject of a sentence (this subject is in general a personal pronouns, like seen previously).

In French, you will find a set of three regular verbs whose terminations are repeating again and again. Remembering the patterns of each one will be very useful. Indeed, verbs finishing in *-er*, *-ir* and *-re* are following a specific pattern that never change most part of time. Those verbs are called "regular verbs". Once you have mastered the three patterns of regular verbs, you will notice that it is much simpler to communicate but also to write! Regular -er, -re and -ir verbs have their own different end patterns, but they are not really difficult to handle, even though they differ from each other. Please note, even if regular verbs are used to cover many conjugations, it is a good idea to practice the verbs you use most frequently, and to use them as the "regular" verbs in your French grammar.

Conjugation

In beginner French lessons, some basic verbs are very useful for expressing simple sentences, such as the verbs etre (to be) an avoir (to have), the verbs in -ER from the first group, the pronominal verbs, the verbs to go, to come and to do, the verbs in -IR from the second group and some verbs from the 3rd group. The first tense to be familiar with is of course the present tense.

For beginners, willing to express themselves in the past, it's important to know the compound past that is used to tell about past events or past actions. To discuss about future actions, to talk about a project for example, the tense to learn is of course the future. But mastering the present tense is a good beginning.

CONJUGATION OF THE VERBS OF THE FIRST GROUP (-ER)

But to start, let's how to conjugate a regular -er verb at the present tense. Most part of the French verbs are verbs ending in -er. It's a good thing for you, because after learning their conjugation pattern in the present tense, you can almost conjugate 80% of French verbs. Amazing, right? In order to conjugate a regular verb ending in -er, you should start by dropping the -er of the infinitive to get the base. Then you just have to add the six present tense endings specific to this category of verbs (-e, -es, -e, -ons, -ez, -ent). Simple! This table displays the conjugation of the verb **aimer** (**to love**) at the present tense.

AIMER / TO LOVE	
FRENCH	**ENGLISH**
J'aime	I love
Tu aime**s**	You love
Il/elle/on aime	He/she love
Nous aim**ons**	We love
Vous aim**ez**	You love
Ils/elles aim**ent**	They love

CONJUGATION OF THE VERBS OF THE SECOND GROUP (-IR)

Verbs ending in -ir are verbs from the second group. It's the second most common type of verb. To create the present tense, drop the -ir of the infinitive to get the base, then add the present tense terminations specific to this type of verbs (-is, -is, -is, -is, -it, -issons, -issez, -issez, -issent). The table below conjugates the verb **finir** (*to finish*).

FINIR / TO FINISH	
FRENCH	**ENGLISH**

Je fini**s**	I finish
Tu fini**s**	You finish
Il/elle/on fini**t**	He/she finishes
Nous finiss**ons**	We finish
Vous finiss**ez**	You finish
Ils/elles finiss**ent**	They finish

Please note, all verbs ending in **-ir** are not following this pattern. So be careful, even if most part of the verbs would use those terminations described above, some exceptions exist.

CONJUGATION OF THE VERBS OF THE SECOND GROUP (-RE)

Verbs ending in -re are verbs from the third group. To create the present tense, drop the -re of the infinitive to get the base, then add the present tense terminations specific to this type of verbs (**-s, -s,** nothing, **-ons, -ez, -ent**). The table below conjugates the verb **vendre** (*to sell*).

VENDRE / TO SELL	
FRENCH	**ENGLISH**
Je vend**s**	I sell
Tu vend**s**	You sell
Il/elle/on vend	He/she sells
Nous vend**ons**	We sell
Vous vend**ez**	You sell
Ils/elles vend**ent**	They sell

Common Irregular French Verbs

As you know now, some verbs are irregular and do not follow the traditional patterns described above. It's the reason why this book is going to teach you the most populars irregulars verbs, to help you to identify and conjugate them. You will find below some models of irregular verbs that you might encounter as you learn French.

ALLER / TO GO	
FRENCH	**ENGLISH**
Je vais	I go
Tu vas	You go
Il/elle/on va	He/she goes
Nous allons	We go
Vous allez	You go
Ils/elles vont	They go

AVOIR / TO HAVE	
FRENCH	**ENGLISH**

J'ai	I have
Tu as	You have
Il/elle/on a	He/she has
Nous avons	We have
Vous avez	You have
Ils/elles ont	They have

DIRE / TO SAY

FRENCH	ENGLISH
Je dis	I say
Tu dis	You say
Il/elle/on dit	He/she says
Nous disons	We say
Vous dites	You say
Ils/elles disent	They say

FAIRE / TO DO

FRENCH	ENGLISH
Je fais	I do
Tu fais	You do
Il/elle/on fait	He/she does
Nous faisons	We do
Vous faites	You do
Ils/elles font	They do

ETRE / TO BE

FRENCH	ENGLISH
Je suis	I am
Tu es	You are
Il/elle/on est	He/she is
Nous sommes	We are
Vous êtes	You are
Ils/elles sont	They are

POUVOIR / TO BE ABLE

FRENCH	ENGLISH
Je peux	I can
Tu peux	You can
Il/elle/on peut	He/she can
Nous pouvons	We can
Vous pouvez	You can
Ils/elles peuvent	They can

SAVOIR / TO KNOW

FRENCH	ENGLISH
Je sais	I know
Tu sais	You know
Il/elle/on sait	He/she know
Nous savons	We know
Vous savez	You know
Ils/elles savent	They know

VOIR / TO SEE

FRENCH	ENGLISH
Je vois	I see
Tu vois	You see
Il/elle/on voit	He/she sees
Nous voyons	We see
Vous voyez	You see
Ils/elles voient	They see

VOULOIR / TO WANT TO	
FRENCH	**ENGLISH**
Je veux	I want
Tu veux	You want
Il/elle/on veut	He/she wants
Nous voulons	We want
Vous voulez	You want
Ils/elles veulent	They want

PRENDRE / TO TAKE	
FRENCH	**ENGLISH**
Je prends	I take
Tu prends	You take
Il/Elle prend	He/She takes
Nous prenons	We take
Vous prenez	You take
Ils/Elles prennent	They take

The endings of the verb **prendre**, are adopted by the following verbs in an identical way:

apprendre (to learn), entreprendre (to undertake), comprendre (to understand), reprendre (to retake), méprendre (to mistake), surprendre (to surprise).

METTRE / TO PUT	
FRENCH	**ENGLISH**
Je mets	I put
Tu mets	You put
Il/Elle met	He/She puts
Nous mettons	We put
Vous mettez	You put
Ils/Elles mettent	They put

The endings of the verb **mettre**, are adopted by the following verbs in an identical way: **admettre** (to admit), **commettre** (to commit), **transmettre** (to transmit), **permettre** (to allow), **soumettre** (to submit), **remettre** (to postpone).

TENIR / TO HOLD

FRENCH	ENGLISH
Je tiens	I hold
Tu tiens	You hold
Il/elle/on tient	He/she holds
Nous tenons	We hold
Vous tenez	You hold
Ils/elles tiennent	They hold

TENIR / TO HOLD	
FRENCH	**ENGLISH**
Je viens	I come
Tu viens	You come
Il/Elle vient	He/She comes
Nous venons	We come
Vous venez	You come
Ils/Elles viennent	They come

The endings of the verb **tenir** and **venir**, are adopted by the following verbs in an identical way: **advenir** (to happen), **abstenir** (to refrain), **advenir** (to happen), **appartenir** (to belong to), **contenir** (to contain), **détenir** (to detain), **convenir** (to suit), **détenir** (to detain), **entretenir** (to support), **devenir** (to become), **maintenir** (to maintain), **parvenir** (to reach), **obtenir** (to obtain), **prévenir** (to warn), **soutenir** (to support), **retenir** (to retain), **subvenir** (to provide), **tenir** (to hold), **survenir** (to occur).

MANGER / TO HOLD	
FRENCH	**ENGLISH**
Je mange	I eat
Tu manges	You eat
Il/elle/on mange	He/she eats
Nous mangeons	We eat
Vous mangez	You eat
Ils/elles mangent	They eat

Verbs finishing in **-ger** have a specific spelling. You have to keep an extra **-e** after the **-g** in order to keep the **"g"** soft. Those verbs are following the same pattern: **changer** (to change), **décourager** (to discourage), **corriger** (to correct), **déménager** (to move), **diriger** (to direct), **déranger** (to disturb), **encourager** (to encourage), **exiger** (to demand), **engager** (to bind), **loger** (to lodge), **juger** (to judge), **mélanger** (to mix), **obliger** (to force), **nager** (to swim), **rédiger** (to write), **partager** (to share), **voyager** (to travel).

LANCER / TO THROW	
FRENCH	**ENGLISH**
Je lance	I throw
Tu lances	You throw
Il/elle/on lance	He/she throws
Nous lançons	We throw
Vous lancez	You throw
Ils/elles lancent	They throw

Verbs ending in **-cer** like **lancer** also have a specific spelling. The **-c** turns into to a **-ç** to keep a soft **"c"** sound : **avancer** (to advance), **annoncer** (to announce), **dénoncer** (to denounce), **commencer** (to commence), **effacer** (to erase), **menacer** (to threaten), **prononcer** (to pronounce), **placer** (to put), **remplacer** (to replace), **renoncer** (to renounce).

PAYER / TO PAY	
FRENCH	**ENGLISH**
Je paie	I pay
Tu paies	You pay
Il/elle/on paie	He/she pays
Nous payons	We pay
Vous payez	You pay
Ils/elles paient	They pay

Verbs finishing in **-yer** like payer ave the **-y** turning into an **-i** in the following forms: je, tu, il, and ils. Those vers are following the same pattern: **aboyer** (to bark), **effrayer** (to frighten), **balayer** (to sweep), **envoyer** (to send), **s'ennuyer** (to be bored), **essuyer** (to wipe), **essayer** (to try), **nettoyer** (to clean), **renvoyer** (to send back), **payer** (to pay).

APPELER / TO CALL	
FRENCH	**ENGLISH**
J'appelle Tu appelles Il/elle/on appelle Nous appelons Vous appelez Ils/elles appellent	I call You call He/she calls We call You call They call

Finally, verbs like **appeler** have to double their final consonant in the following forms: je, tu, il, and ils. These verbs are following the same pattern : **épeler** (to spell out), **appeler** (to call), **étinceler** (to sparkle), **jeter** (to jump), **renouveler** (to renew).

Those tables will help you to get a quick understanding of the conjugations pattern for variable and invariable verbs.

Remember, working on your daily skills is an excellent way to learn French grammar and conjugation and move faster to the next level of language fluency.

Past: Perfect Tense (*Passé Composé*)

Regular Verbs

The perfect tense is essentially a compound tense which means, as you probably understood, is composed of more than one part. In French in order to create the perfect tense, you have to use the verb *être* (to be) or *avoir* (to have). You need to learn the present tense to create the Passé Composé and the conjugations of these two verbs specifically. The verb avoir is in general the most commonly used. We will study the verb être later on. As example we will study the verb *aider* (to help). This verb needs the auxiliary avoir in order to create the past perfect tense. As you know the conjugation of avoir in the present tense is the following one:

J'ai (I have)

Tu as (You have)

Il / Elle a (He / she has)

Nous avons (We have)

Vous avez (You have)

Ils / Elles ont (They have)

Now you know the conjugation of the auxiliary verb *avoir*, you need to add the past participle. Follow this pattern below to figure out what the past participle. This pattern is designed for regular verbs, we will get to irregular verbs later on.

- For verbs ending in -er , like *manger* (to eat), *nager* (to swim), *danser* (to danse), etc. drop the ''-er'' and replace it with -é to to create the past participle: *mangé, nagé, dansé.*
- For verbs ending in -ir like *partir* (to leave), *finir* (to finish), *choisir* (to choose), etc. you have to drop the ''-ir'' and replace it with –i to create the past participle: *parti, fini, choisi.*
- For verbs ending in –re like *attendre* (to wait), *survivre* (to survive), *répondre* (to respond), etc. drop the –re and replace it with -u to create the past participle: *attendu, survécu, répondu.*

So as a result, the perfect tense is:

First the helping auxiliary verb + Second the past participle = The perfect tense.

If you do it right, it should look like this: *J'ai dansé* (I danced). *Tu as mangé* (You swam). *Il a choisi* (He choosed). *Elle a réfléchi* (She thought). *Nous avons attendu* (We waited). *Vous avez répondu* (You answered). *Ils ont survécu* (They survived). *Elles ont nagé* (They swimmed).

Now that we've reviewed the general rule, let's take a look at the common struggles you might face with the perfect tense, and we will tell you how to overcome them.

Irregular Verbs

Now you understood how to use the perfect tense you should be able to use it with not too much difficulties. Also, as much as we hate it, you have to know that it's not that simple. Indeed, there are actual irregular past participles that you need to learn in order to master the perfect tense.

If you follow the pattern of past participles described earlier without thinking twice, with verbs like comprendre (to understand), *faire* (to do), *être* (to be), *avoir* (to have), or *boire* (to drink), then you will end up with some made-up words like: comprendu, fairu, etu... Those aren't real words, and it's the reason why you need to know, at least the most commons irregular past participles out there. You will find below some of the most common verbs and their past participles. Once again most of them use *avoir* as their auxiliary helping verb. We organized them according their ending to help you to memorize them.

The small "u" group:

VERBS	PAST PARTICIPLES
Pleuvoir (to rain)	Plu
Avoir (to have)	Eu
Devoir (to have to)	Dû
Savoir (to know)	Su
Pouvoir (to be able to)	Pu
Boire (to drink)	Bu
Croire (to believe)	Cru

Lire (to read)	Lu
Voir (to see)	Vu

The Double "u" group:

VERBS	PAST PARTICIPLES
Vivre (to live)	Vécu
Recevoir (to receive)	Reçu
Connaître (to know)	Connu
Courir (to run)	Couru
Vouloir (to want)	Voulu
Venir (to come)	Venu

The "-is" Group:

VERBS	PAST PARTICIPLES
Comprendre (to understand)	Compris
Mettre (to put)	Mis
Apprendre (to learn)	Appris
Prendre (to take)	Pris

The "-it" Group:

VERBS	PAST PARTICIPLES
Ecrire (to write)	Ecrit
Dire (to say)	Dit
Conduire (to drive)	Conduit

The "-ert" Group:

VERBS	PAST PARTICIPLES
Souffrir (to suffer)	Souffert
Ouvrir (to open)	Ouvert
Découvrir (to discover)	Découvert
Couvrir (to cover)	Couvert
Offrir (to offer)	Offert

The Odd Ones: Être (to be) – été. Faire (to do,make) – fait.

Tip: This tip is not working everytime but in order to know if your verb is regular or irregular, you should try the following corresponding endings : –*é, -i,* or –*u*. If it looks weird or hard to pronounce because you end up with too many vowels in a row, it might means that the participle is irregular.

The second helping auxiliary verb: *Être*

Remember we mentioned early two types of helping auxiliary verbs: ***avoir*** and ***être***. Well even if you might have to use avoir most oftenly, you need to know the verbs using the helping auxiliary verb être. You will find below a list of the most common used verbs using the helping auxiliary verb être, with the right past participles and their meanings.

VERBS	PAST PARTICIPLES
Arriver (to arrive)	Arrivé
Retourner (to return)	Retourné
Tomber (to fall)	Tombé
Rentrer (to go back)	Rentré
Entrer (to enter)	Entré
Descendre (to go down)	Descendu
Naître (to be born)	Né
Venir (to come)	Venu
Aller (to go)	Allé
Venir (to come)	Venu
Sortir (to go out)	Sorti
Rester (to stay)	Resté
Monter (to go up)	Monté
Revenir (to come back)	Revenu
Devenir (to become)	Devenu
Mourir (to die)	Mort
Partir (to leave)	Parti

All of these verbs are movement verbs as you probably noticed (going, coming, arriving, leaving, etc), except the verbs *naître* and *mourir*. Remember it, when you wonder which helping verbs you need between *avoir* and *être*. this in mind when you're rattling your brain to remember which helping verb you need. Most part of the past participles involving the helping verb *être* are regulars.

So like the verb avoir you need to conjugate the verb *être* to the present tense: *Je suis, Tu es, Il/Elle est, Nous sommes, Vous êtes, Ils/Elles sont;* and you add your past participle just like shown before. For instance: *Je suis sorti, tu es parti, il est revenu, etc.*

Now it's time to overcome the struggle inherent to the conjugation of the past compound associated to the verb to be. Indeed, when you use the helper auxiliary verb *être* (to be) you have to agree the past participle with its subject. It's the main struggle you will have to overcome regarding the helper verb "*être*". As you understood by now the gender agreements in French is a serious business. For instance, the verb *partir* (to leave) should be conjugated as it follows:

Je suis allé(e).

Tu es allé(e).

Il est allé / Elle est allée.

Nous sommes allé(e)s.

Vous êtes allé(e)s.

Ils sont allés / Elles sont allé(e)s.

As you might noticed, you need to add a "*-e*" at the past participle if the subject is feminine. And a "*-s*" if the subject is plural. And of course it will be "*-es*" if the subject is feminine plural.

Verbs that can use *Être* or *Avoir*.

You will face situation when *être* like *avoir* can be used as helper verbs. But according the helper verb you pick, your sentence will end up meaning something completely different. Once you will be able to use the right helper verb you will sound like a real pro. Indeed, verbs like *monter, descendre, retourner, passer, rentrer* or *sortir* should be traditionally use with the verb *être* but depending the context it can be used with the verb *avoir*. *Monter, descendre, retourner, passer, rentrer* or *sortir* are motion verbs. But those verbs can have different meanings non related with moving. So which helping verbs are you supposed to use? It will all depend on the direct object in the sentence. A direct object, if you already forgot, is the piece of sentence completing the verb and giving extra information about it. Let's take a look, with the verb **retourner**:

Retourner, with *Être*: *Elle est retournée <u>en France</u>.* (She went back in France.)

Note we added an "e" because the helper verb here is être, and we need to agree the past participle with the subject : elle (she), which is feminine singular. The direct object is en France (in France). It's a location, so the verb implies a motion.

Retourner with Avoir: *Elle a retourné <u>la crêpe dans la poêle</u>.* (She flipped out the crepe into the stove).

Note we didn't add any extra "e" at the end of the past participle. There's no gender or number agreement with the helper verb *avoir*. In this case the direct object is: *la crêpe dans la poêle* (the crepe into the stove). It implies something different that a motion and as you seen the sentence meaning is there, completely different.

You will find below some other examples:

Passer

With *Être*: *Elles sont passées par la maison.* (They passed by the house).

With *Avoir*: *Elles ont passé un bon séjour.* (They spent a good stay).

Monter

With *Être: Je suis monté au premier étage.* (I went up to the first floor).

With *Avoir: J'ai monté ce meuble.* (I put this piece of furniture together).

Rentrer

With *Être: Tu es rentré hier.* (You came yesterday).

With *Avoir: Tu as rentré ton vélo dans le garage.* (You put back your bike in the garage).

Retourner

With *Être: Ils sont retournés chez le docteur.* (They returned to the doctor).

With *Avoir: Ils ont retourné le coussin.* (They turned over the pillow).

Sortir

With *Être: Nous sommes sortis.* (We went out)

Avec *Avoir: Nous avons sorti le chat.* (We put the cat out).

It might seem complicated but an everyday practice should help you to figure this specificity out. And now get ready for another struggle:

Case where the helper verb *avoir* agrees

We seen that when you use the helping verb *être* the participle must agrees with the subject, but if you use *avoir*, it doesn't. Easy right? Well, it would not be french without EXCEPTION.

Once again, under specific circumstances, the participle used with the helper verb *avoir* **must agree**. It can sound overwhelming, but we are going to help you to overcome this little struggle. Promise.

We talked earlier about direct object. The placement of the direct object is the circumstance affecting the agreement between the participle and the subject. First let's talk about when the direct object becomes a direct object <u>pronoun</u>. This direct object pronoun replaces the direct object and is placed BEFORE the verb. For instance: *J'ai vu un chat* (I saw a cat) becomes: *Je l'ai vu* (I saw it). Here *l'* is the direct object pronoun and replaces "un chat".

Like l'; le, la or les can be object pronouns. It goes before the verb and force you to agree your participle with the direct pronoun. In other word, the past participle must agree with one thing: the direct object pronoun. In the sentence displayed above, the direct object pronoun "le chat" is masculine singular, it's the reason why it doesn't change the ending of the past participle. But for instance, if the sentence was: *J'ai vu les chats* (I saw the cats). It would become: *Je **les** ai vu**s*** (I saw them). In short, it agrees!

The case of the reflexive Verbs

We already explained earlier in this book what were the reflexive verbs. You might wonder why we are talking about it again now. With no surprise, they do exist at the present tense as well and by chance, they are relatively easy to create. But of course, French would not be French without some weird specificities.

Creating Reflexive Verbs, case of the Perfect Tense:

Reflexive verbs concerned only the verb *être*, and they always agree with their subject. Just like non reflexive verbs using the helper verb *être* at the perfect tense. For instance:

- *Je me suis couché (I went to bed)* - In a literal way: I layed myself down to bed.
- *Tu t'es endormi.* (You fell asleep).
- *Il s'est amusé.* (He had fun).
- *Elle s'est énervée.* (She got angry).
- *Nous nous sommes brossés les cheveux.* (We brushed our hair).
- *Vous vous êtes maquillées.* (You put makeup on).
- *Ils se sont rasés.* (They shaved).
- *Elles se sont réveillées.* (They woke up).

Basically it is like the other verbs, but with the little reflexive pronoun that precedes the helper verb. The most important thing is to keep in mind that the reflexive pronoun always agrees with the subject. But like we said, there's a small catch. This catch shows up when the reflexive verb is directly followed by a body part. Yes, you seen right : a body part. In that case, and only in that case the past participle doesn't agree. For instance:
-*Elles se sont lavé les pieds.* (They washed their feet).
-*Elle s'est cassé le bras.* (She broke her arm)
As you seen, in those sentences above, the past participles don't agree. So try to remember this weird body part exception in mind when it's time to agree your verb with its subject.
The perfect tense can seem complicated but once you will understand its exceptions and how to overcome the struggles

then you will be able to master this tense. The most important thing is to remember the general rules, the irregulars verbs, but also the agreement rules and its exceptions. Once it will be done, good news: you officially have the finesse of a native French speaker!

We know this tense can be complicated, but it's very important to learn it. Once you did, you will realize how much the other compound tenses are now easy to study.

Common phrases used by traveler

Traveling to France is a wonderful journey where you will have the chance to experience local culture, as well as all the beautiful artwork and exquisite cuisine! As you are getting ready for your trip, it is essential that you try to learn some new languages skills. If you are interested by the common phrases used by travellers, please keep reading. It will help you to navigate throughout France and any french-speaking territory with ease. Remember, the best way to experience your journey is to immerse yourself completely by talking with the local population. We hope this section will give you many opportunities to practice your French.

Standard conversational sentences in French	
Bonjour! Bonsoir!	Hello! Good evening!
Bienvenue.	Welcome.
Madame, mademoiselle, monsieur.	Madam, miss, sir.
Excuse- moi.	Excuse me.
Je ne parle pas francais.	I don't speak French
Parlez-vous anglais?	Do you speak English?
Merci beaucoup.	Thank you very much.
De rien.	You're welcome.
A plus tard.	See you later.

GETTING INFORMATION	
Pourriez-vous m'aider?	Could you help me?
Je ne comprends pas.	I don't understand.
Parlez lentement, s'il vous plaît.	Speak slowly, please.
Répétez, s'il vous plaît.	Repeat, please.
Où sont les toilettes ?	Where are the toilets?
Où puis-je trouver un bon restaurant?	Where can I found a good restaurant?
Où se trouve (la ville, la plage, la rue St Michel...)?	Where is (the city, the beach, St Michel street...)?
Je cherche (le métro, la gare, l'aéroport...) ?	I'm looking for (the metro, the train station, the airport...)?
Je cherche (l'hôtel x, la police, le distributeur...).	I'm looking for (the hotel x, the police, the atm...).
Pourriez-vous nous prendre en photo?	Could you take us in photo?

ASKING FOR DIRECTIONS

C'est tout droit	It's straight away.
C'est sur la gauche.	It's to the left.
C'est sur la droite.	It's to the right.
C'est loin ? C'est proche ?	Is it far? Is it close?
Où sommes-nous ?	Where are we?

TRANSPORTATION	
Puis-je regarder les horaires?	Can I look at the schedule?
Puis-je réserver un billet ?	Can I reserve a ticket?
Puis-je acheter un billet aller simple/aller-retour ?	Can I purchase a one-way ticket/a round-trip ticket?
A quelle heure doit-il arriver ?	At what time should it arrive?

HOTEL	
Avez-vous une chambre disponible?	Do you have a room available?
Avez-vous la climatisation?	Do you have air conditioning?
Avez-vous une chambre disponible?	Do you have a double room?
Puis-je annuler ma réservation ?	Can I cancel my booking?
Quand est le check-out ?	When is the check-out?

SHOPPING	
Où est le centre commercial?	Where is the mall?
Où sont les magasins ?	Where are the shops?
Acceptez-vous les cartes de crédit ?	Do you accept credit card?
A quelle heure ouvrez vous ?	At what time do you open?
A quelle heure fermez vous ?	At what time do you close?
Je cherche (un livre, une robe, une carte...).	I am looking for a (book, dress, card...).
Combien cela coûte-t-il ?	How much does it cost?
C'est une bonne affaire.	It's a great deal.
C'est trop cher.	It's too expensive.
C'est génial/mauvais	It's great/bad

RESTAURANT	
Je voudrais (un café, de l'eau, une bière, un verre de vin, un jus, un thé...).	I would like (a coffee, water, a beer, a glass of wine, a juice, a tea....).
Le menu, s'il vous plaît.	The menu, please.
La note, s'il vous plaît.	The bill, please.
Puis-je réserver une table pour ce soir ?	Can I book a table for tonight?
C'est délicieux, merci.	It's delicious, thank you.

Conclusion

Learning a foreign language is not an easy task, and it will take a huge commitment
from you to become even somewhat proficient in French. Some studies suggest that communicating in another language comes after few years of arduous study, while others claim that under the right conditions it can be picked up much sooner. However, any individual who intends to become fluent in a foreign language will truly have to work for it. In order to keep such a commitment, there are certain measures that need to be taken. The most notable involves scheduling, which means that you must organize your daily activities so that they include some French study and practice time. Besides scheduling, another step you can take is to work on your self-motivation. This involves rewarding yourself for any language learning successes or accomplishments. This may mean eating your favorite meal after completing a tough French lesson or perhaps buying something you'd like if you score high on a test. Motivation is the primary force behind learning, so you should always take time out to recognize and praise your own language growth. Still another step toward making the commitment to learning French is having outside support. Since it takes years to develop good communication skills, you will need

family, maybe teachers or friends to encourage you along the way. You can also benefit from the help of a personal tutor or an enthusiastic group of fellow learners, in order to overcome barriers to fluency. Securing loyal supporters is an essential key to become better in French. Another secret to staying committed is making sure you know exactly what your ultimate goal is. Though you may take measures to stay on course, questions about your final objective might still remain. "What will I do with the French I'm learning? "How far do I plan to go? "Why am I learning French anyway?" These are all legitimate concerns that help determine one's commitment level. Once you know what you are shooting for, the job will become a lot less stressful. Also, be sure to ask yourself how much you really enjoy the French language. People need to like the language they are learning and at least some aspects of its culture if they plan on studying it for a while. One final area of commitment for French learners is time spent on the Internet, simply because the Internet now offers a wide range of content and learning materials.

There are numerous free or low-cost websites with excellent learning tools, apps, online tutors, and even access to folks from French-speaking countries with whom speak and interact. The Internet is a virtual classroom, library, bookstore, language laboratory, and support community. It is the home of the language-learning revolution, and now, with our advances in technology, the Internet is available wherever and whenever we want it, at no or very little cost. Without question, learning French takes plenty of self-discipline and personal sacrifice. Scheduling, finding ways to stay motivated, seeking support, setting goals, and spending time on the Internet are all required if you truly are committed to become fluent in French. But remember, feeling comfortable around people from French-speaking countries will make a difference. The more you know about the French culture, the closer you'll be to understanding their language. If you struggle with self-confidence, try to unwind before you say anything. Apply any stress-relief or relaxation techniques prior to conversing in deep breath, giggle, and then just go for it. Assertive, outgoing students usually pick up French faster than others. So, try to guess, take chances, and experiment whenever you are unsure. Commit to practicing French every single day-without fail. Whether its searching online, trying a new greeting, or calling out items throughout the house, try to review and improve every chance you get! Bear in mind that being close in grammar and pronunciation is usually good enough. Folks will understand you as long as the key words are there, so avoid stopping to translate every little detail during a conversation. Roll with the general.

We hope that this manual will become the cornerstone of your apprenticeship and will allow you to develop your French knowledge through these different sections. However, remember that it is necessary to build your knowledge at home and practice a little every day.

CPSIA information can be obtained
at www.ICGtesting.com
Printed in the USA
BVHW091344021220
594477BV00018B/954